DEFENDING DOUBLED CONTRACTS

You have doubled the opposition contract and now must find the best path to inflict maximum damage. Is the contract a close thing so that you must ensure that you do actually defeat the contract? Have the opponents sacrificed against your game, which would have succeeded? In that case, not only do you need to defeat their contract, but must strive to produce a result where the penalties you receive are adequate compensation for the game you would have made.

These are the sort of questions that will face you in this quiz book of bridge problems. The deals all come from actual play. Most of them arose in major national and international championships. In most cases you have the chance to do better than the defenders did at the table. As long as you tackle the problems with zeal and determination, your own defence is bound to improve, even if you do not find the best answer every time.

Ron Klinger is a leading international bridge teacher and has represented Australia in many world championships since 1976. He has written over sixty books, some of which have been translated into Bulgarian, Chinese, Danish, French, Hebrew and Icelandic. He has written a daily bridge column in *The Sydney Morning Herald* and *The Sun-Herald* for over twelve years. He provides material for the quizzes and problems on the www.ronklingerbridge.com website and contributes regularly to a number of bridge magazines.

By RON KLINGER *in the Master Bridge Series*

BASIC BRIDGE: *The Guide to Good Acol Bidding and Play*
BETTER BRIDGE WITH A BETTER MEMORY • BRIDGE IS FUN
THE POWER OF SHAPE • WHEN TO BID, WHEN TO PASS
*GUIDE TO BETTER CARD PLAY • PLAYING TO WIN AT BRIDGE
GUIDE TO BETTER ACOL BRIDGE • 20 GREAT CONVENTIONS FLIPPER
GUIDE TO BETTER DUPLICATE BRIDGE • TEACH YOUR CHILD BRIDGE
BRIDGE CONVENTIONS, DEFENCES AND COUNTERMEASURES
100 WINNING BRIDGE TIPS • 50 MORE WINNING BRIDGE TIPS
100 WINNING DUPLICATE TIPS • ACOL BRIDGE MADE EASY
THE MODERN LOSING TRICK COUNT • IMPROVE YOUR BRIDGE MEMORY
IMPROVE YOUR DECLARER PLAY AT NO-TRUMPS
IMPROVE YOUR PLAY AT TRUMP CONTRACTS
IMPROVE YOUR OPENING LEADS • IMPROVE YOUR SLAM BIDDING
RON KLINGER'S MASTER CLASS • 5-CARD MAJOR STAYMAN
RON KLINGER ANSWERS YOUR BRIDGE QUERIES
BASIC ACOL BRIDGE FLIPPER • ACOL BRIDGE FLIPPER
DUPLICATE BRIDGE FLIPPER • MODERN LOSING TRICK COUNT FLIPPER
MEMORY-AIDS AND USEFUL RULES FLIPPER
BID BETTER, MUCH BETTER AFTER OPENING 1 NO-TRUMP
TO WIN AT BRIDGE • †RIGHT THROUGH THE PACK AGAIN
PLAYING DOUBLED CONTRACTS • DEFENDING DOUBLED CONTRACTS

*Winner of the 1991 Book of the Year Award of the American Bridge Teachers' Association
†Winner of the 2009 International Bridge Press Association Book of the Year Award

with Andrew Kambites
UNDERSTANDING THE UNCONTESTED AUCTION
UNDERSTANDING SLAM BIDDING
HOW GOOD IS YOUR BRIDGE HAND?
CARD PLAY MADE EASY 3: *Trump Management*

with Hugh Kelsey
NEW INSTANT GUIDE TO BRIDGE

with Mike Lawrence
OPENING LEADS FOR ACOL PLAYERS
OPENING LEADS FLIPPER

with Derek Rimington
IMPROVE YOUR BIDDING AND PLAY

with David Jackson
BETTER BALANCED BIDDING

with Roger Trézel and Terence Reese
THE MISTAKES YOU MAKE AT BRIDGE

with Wladyslaw Izdebski and Roman Krzemien
DEADLY DEFENCE • THE DEADLY DEFENCE QUIZ BOOK

with Wladyslaw Izdebski, Dariusz Kardas and Wlodzimierz Krysztofczyk
THE POWER OF POSITIVE BIDDING

DEFENDING DOUBLED CONTRACTS

Ron Klinger

IN ASSOCIATION WITH
PETER CRAWLEY

First published in Great Britain 2016
in association with Peter Crawley
by Weidenfeld & Nicolson
an imprint of the Orion Publishing Group Ltd
Carmelite House, 50 Victoria Embankment, London EC4Y 0DZ

an Hachette UK Company

1 3 5 7 9 10 8 6 4 2

A CIP catalogue record for this book is available from the British Library.

ISBN 978 1 474 60068 2

Typeset by Modern Bridge Publications
P.O. Box 140, Northbridge NSW 1560, Australia

Printed in Great Britain by
Clays Ltd, St Ives plc

The Orion Publishing Group's policy is to use papers that are natural,
renewable and recyclable products and made from wood grown in sustainable
forests. The logging and manufacturing processes are expected to conform to
the environmental regulations of the country of origin.

www.orionbooks.co.uk

Contents

Introduction

Oh, it's fun to collect penalties, but how much more fun to collect bigger penalties. 'Greed is good.' Why be satisfied with 500 when you could have collected 800 or 1100? This book will show you how to make the most of your opportunities for penalties.

This is not a book to be read through in one go. Rather tackle one, two or three problems a day. There are no set themes. Just as at the bridge table, you have to deal with each situation as it arises. Some problems are relatively easy. Some are quite tough. Your aim could be to make sure the contract is defeated or your objective might be to collect enough in penalties to compensate you for the game you would have made.

The contracts range from the one-level to the seven-level. The penalties you can achieve are from one down to six down. None of the problems are composed. They all arose in actual bridge games. Many of them are from international or national tournaments. The players were all experts, in theory anyway. On most of the deals you are challenged to do better than the players did at the table. On some occasions you will impress yourself if you actually match the performance of the players in real life. You might also be impressed by the skill of these defenders.

Unless stated otherwise, assume the problems are set at teams' play or at Imps. The clues you have can be found in the auction and the early play. If partner is the one who doubled, it will pay you to focus on the values partner should have to justify the double and partner's other bidding. You will find a lot of material on signalling, some of which might be new to you. There are also ideas about signalling itself, with which you might not yet be familiar. One thing is for sure. Doing the problems in this book is bound to sharpen your defence and since defence is a partnership matter, make sure partner acquires a copy of this book, too.

Ron Klinger, 2016

1. Dealer North : North-South vulnerable

♠ A 10 7 4
♥ 10 8 5
♦ K Q 10 3
♣ J 3

♠ Q 9 5 2
♥ A K 9 4 3
♦ ---
♣ A 10 9 2

West	North	East	South
	Pass	Pass	1♦
1♥	Double (1)	2♦ (2)	2♠
4♥	4♠	Double	All pass

(1) Exactly four spades   (2) Good heart raise

Trick 1: ♥A: 5 – 2 – 7. Trick 2: ♥K: 8 – 6 – J. What next?
Solution on page 10.

2. Dealer North : North-South vulnerable

♠ 6 4 2
♥ K 6 5
♦ J 8 2
♣ 10 7 5 2

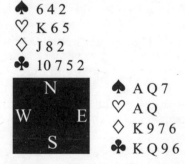

♠ A Q 7
♥ A Q
♦ K 9 7 6
♣ K Q 9 6

South opened 1NT, 12-14, Pass : Pass to East, who doubled to show a strong hand. It went Pass : Pass to North, who redoubled. East passed and South removed to 2♣, 3+ clubs. This was passed to East, who doubled for penalties, all pass. West led the ♣4: two – queen – ace. South played the ♥10: seven (natural count) – five – queen. What should East do now?   *Solution on page 11.*

1. Round 6, Board 22, 2012 World Transnational Mixed Teams:

Contract: 4♠ doubled
Lead: ♡A

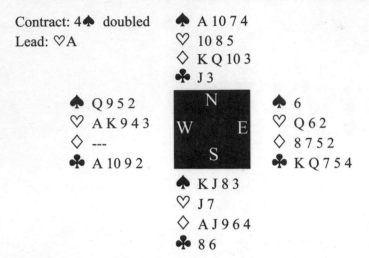

```
              ♠ A 10 7 4
              ♡ 10 8 5
              ◇ K Q 10 3
              ♣ J 3
♠ Q 9 5 2                      ♠ 6
♡ A K 9 4 3          N         ♡ Q 6 2
◇ ---            W       E     ◇ 8 7 5 2
♣ A 10 9 2           S         ♣ K Q 7 5 4
              ♠ K J 8 3
              ♡ J 7
              ◇ A J 9 6 4
              ♣ 8 6
```

It should be clear to play a club at trick 3. It is dangerous to play a third heart. That would give South a chance to shine. South could ruff with the ♠8 and lead the ♠J. Whether West covers or not, declarer can draw trumps and come to four spades, a heart ruff and five diamonds for +790. In the 2012 Transnational, no South found that play when West did play a third heart.

East has also given you a strong clue. East began with ♡Q-6-2. Without the ♣K, East could play ♡6, then ♡2. Both West and East know there is no third heart trick for the defence. Thus East plays ♡2 with club strength and ♡6, then ♡2 without club values.

If West plays ♣A and then ♣9, East can switch to a diamond. West ruffs for +500. If West trusts East enough, West can play a low club. East wins with the ♣Q and returns a diamond (else why would West not cash ♣A first?). Another club to East and another diamond ruff gives East-West 800. Some pairs achieved that. For even more, how about ♡A, then ♡9 if the ♡2 is encouraging? East wins and returns the ◇2. Then diamond ruff, club to ♣Q, diamond ruff, club to ♣K and a third diamond ruff for +1100.

2. Board 32, World Transnational Mixed Teams final, 2012

Contract: 2♣ doubled
Lead: ♣4

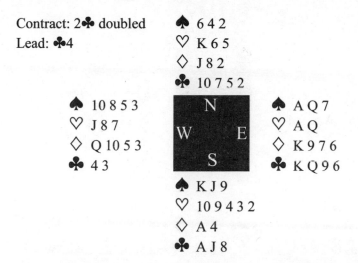

```
              ♠ 6 4 2
              ♡ K 6 5
              ◇ J 8 2
              ♣ 10 7 5 2
♠ 10 8 5 3         N          ♠ A Q 7
♡ J 8 7      W          E     ♡ A Q
◇ Q 10 5 3        S          ◇ K 9 7 6
♣ 4 3                         ♣ K Q 9 6
              ♠ K J 9
              ♡ 10 9 4 3 2
              ◇ A 4
              ♣ A J 8
```

After South won trick 1 and returned the ♡10 to East's queen, the best defence is a switch to diamonds, but that is hard for East to tell. West can have very little and South might have ◇A-Q-x.

East's best move is to cash the ♡A. Regardless of the heart holding, West should give a suit preference signal on this, the ♡7 for the lower suit, diamonds. With something useful in spades, West would play the ♡J, since it is doomed anyway, now that the ♡K has been set up. East should then switch to the ◇6. From that point on, South is destined to go two down on best defence.

At the table East switched to the ♠A at trick 3, cashed the ♡A next and reverted to the ♠7. South won with the ♠J and played the ♣8: three – ten – king. If you place South with ♣A-J-8, South cannot also have ◇A-Q-x as South has shown up with 4 points in spades and is limited to 12-14. There was still time to play a diamond to take the contract one off, but East persevered with the ♠Q. South won, cashed the ♣J and played a heart to the ♡K. Whether East ruffed or discarded, declarer had eight tricks, +180.

3. Dealer South : Both vulnerable

```
            ♠ 8 7 4
            ♡ 10 7 6 2
            ◇ K
            ♣ J 7 6 4 2
```

```
                          ♠ A 5
                          ♡ A K Q
                          ◇ A 9 7 4
                          ♣ K Q 5 3
```

West	North	East	South
			1♠
Pass	2♠	Double	4♠
Pass	Pass	Double	All pass

West leads the ◇8: king – ace – three. What should East do now?

Solution on page 14.

4. Dealer West : Both vulnerable

```
            ♠ A Q 10 7 4
            ♡ K 3 2
            ◇ 9 5 2
            ♣ A 7
```

```
                          ♠ K J 6
                          ♡ A Q 10 4
                          ◇ A 8
                          ♣ K Q 4 3
```

West	North	East	South
3◇	Double	Pass	3♠
Pass	Pass	Double	All pass

West leads the ♣10. Declarer takes the ♣A and returns the ♣7: queen – five – nine. What next?   *Solution on page 15.*

5. Dealer North : East-West vulnerable

```
                    ♠ 10 7 5
                    ♡ Q 10 5 2
                    ◇ K 8 5
                    ♣ 10 8 4

                              ♠ A K Q
                              ♡ 7
                              ◇ A Q
                              ♣ A K Q 9 6 3 2
```

West	North	East	South
	Pass	2♣ (Big)	2♡
2♠	4♡	4NT	6◇
Double	6♡	6♠	Pass
Pass	7♡	Double	All pass

West leads the ♣J. East takes the ♣Q and returns the ♣A. South ruffs and plays the ◇6: nine – five – queen. East plays the ♠K: six – nine (even number) – five. What next?

Solution on page 16.

6. Dealer South : East-West vulnerable

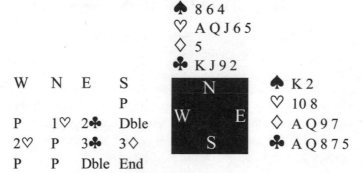

```
                    ♠ 8 6 4
                    ♡ A Q J 6 5
                    ◇ 5
                    ♣ K J 9 2

                              ♠ K 2
                              ♡ 10 8
                              ◇ A Q 9 7
                              ♣ A Q 8 7 5
```

W	N	E	S
			P
P	1♡	2♣	Dble
2♡	P	3♣	3◇
P	P	Dble	End

West leads the ♣3: jack – queen – four. East switches to the ♠K: five – three – four. What next?

Solution on page 17.

3. From the qualifying rounds of a National Open Teams, 2014:

Contract: 4♠ doubled
Lead: ◇8

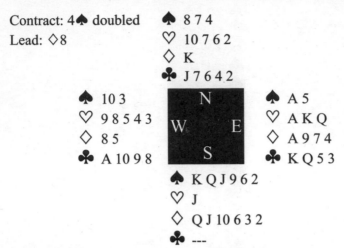

♠ 8 7 4
♡ 10 7 6 2
◇ K
♣ J 7 6 4 2

♠ 10 3
♡ 9 8 5 4 3
◇ 8 5
♣ A 10 9 8

♠ A 5
♡ A K Q
◇ A 9 7 4
♣ K Q 5 3

♠ K Q J 9 6 2
♡ J
◇ Q J 10 6 3 2
♣ ---

In one match both N-S pairs were in 4♠ doubled. At one table, after a lengthy auction, West led the ♡3. East won and shifted to the ♠A and the ♠5. South won, conceded a diamond and claimed ten tricks, +790. There were 35 other 790s for making 4♠ doubled.

At the other table, after the auction given, West led the ◇8, king, ace. Here, too, East switched to ♠A and the ♠5. South won and discarded all of dummy's hearts on the diamond winners. The ♡J was ruffed for eleven tricks, +990 and +5 Imps. There were two other scores of 990 in 4♠ doubled.

The ◇8 could be from Q-10-8 or a singleton or top of a doubleton. Leading a diamond from Q-10-8 is not attractive. West had a safer heart lead. East knows that North-South have bid game vulnerable with at most 18 HCP. Clearly South must have extreme shape. If the ◇8 is top from a doubleton, South will have six diamonds and so probably six spades. East should return the ◇9 at trick 2. When East comes in with the ♠A, the ♡A and a third diamond will defeat 4♠. Playing the ♡A before the third diamond could be wrong, but if East just gives West the ruff, West might try the ♣A.

4. Board 45, Baze Senior Knockoout Teams (USA), 2013

Contract: 3♠ doubled
Lead: ♣10

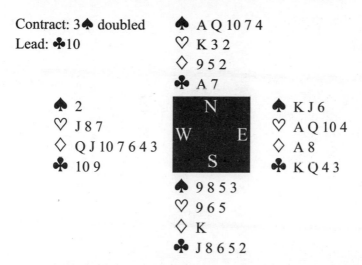

```
               ♠ A Q 10 7 4
               ♡ K 3 2
               ◇ 9 5 2
               ♣ A 7
  ♠ 2              N              ♠ K J 6
  ♡ J 8 7                        ♡ A Q 10 4
  ◇ Q J 10 7 6 4 3   W     E      ◇ A 8
  ♣ 10 9            S            ♣ K Q 4 3
               ♠ 9 8 5 3
               ♡ 9 6 5
               ◇ K
               ♣ J 8 6 5 2
```

The vulnerable 3◇ opening with only five playing tricks would not be a popular choice, one hopes. North's takeout double was no thing of beauty either.

After East wins trick 2 with the ♣Q, it seems automatic to switch to the ◇A. When the ◇K drops, East can continue diamonds or switch to hearts. Either way E-W will come to five or six tricks.

As West had no high card values in either black suit and at most the jack in hearts, East felt West must have the ◇K. Expecting to put West on lead for a heart switch, East played the ◇8 at trick 2. South won and made the most of this unexpected gift.

South played a club, ♠2, ♠7, ruffed a diamond, ruffed a club with the ♠10 and ruffed a diamond, as East discarded the ♡4 (it does not help East to ruff with the ♠J – South discards a heart). South played the club winner and discarded a heart from dummy. East could ruff, but could make only one spade and one heart. Thus 3♠ doubled made. Note that East is one of the world's great players.

5. Round 4, Board 19, Sports Accord World Open Teams, 2014

Contract: 7♡ doubled
Lead: ♣J

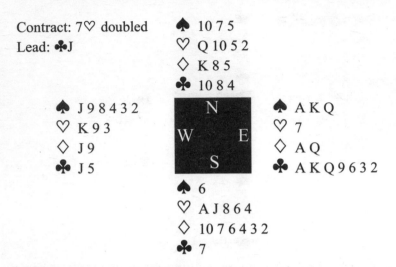

```
                  ♠ 10 7 5
                  ♡ Q 10 5 2
                  ◇ K 8 5
                  ♣ 10 8 4
  ♠ J 9 8 4 3 2         N          ♠ A K Q
  ♡ K 9 3          W         E     ♡ 7
  ◇ J 9                 S          ◇ A Q
  ♣ J 5                            ♣ A K Q 9 6 3 2
                  ♠ 6
                  ♡ A J 8 6 4
                  ◇ 10 7 6 4 3 2
                  ♣ 7
```

After ♣J, taken by the ♣Q, and the ♣A, ruffed by South, East knows that East-West can make 6♣ or 6♠, or seven if West has the ♡A. After South's ◇6 ducked to the queen, East played the ♠K and West's ♠9 showed an even number of spades, obviously six. South is therefore 1-1 in the black suits and, from South's 6◇ bid, South will be 6-5 in the red suits. Which way round will it be?

With six hearts and five clearly trashy diamonds, why would South bother to introduce the diamonds? South would just bid 6♡. Hence South figures to be five hearts and six diamonds and East should continue with a top spade or a top club. In practice East cashed the ◇A. What was the purpose behind that? It set up the diamonds, as South unblocked the king. East reverted to the ♣K. South ruffed with the ♡J and West discarded a spade. Declarer led a low heart and whether West ducked or took the ♡K, South lost only one more trick. That was five down, −1100 for +7 Imps against 6♣ +1370 at the other table. If East plays a spade or a top club after the ♠K, best defence can collect 1400 for +1 Imp.

6. Round 5, Board 12, Sports Accord World Open Teams, 2014

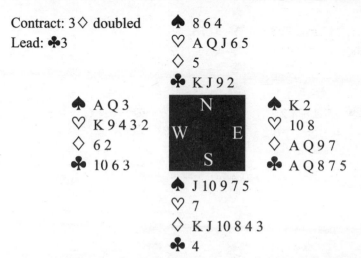

Contract: 3♢ doubled
Lead: ♣3

    ♠ 8 6 4
    ♡ A Q J 6 5
    ♢ 5
    ♣ K J 9 2

♠ A Q 3
♡ K 9 4 3 2
♢ 6 2
♣ 10 6 3

♠ K 2
♡ 10 8
♢ A Q 9 7
♣ A Q 8 7 5

    ♠ J 10 9 7 5
    ♡ 7
    ♢ K J 10 8 4 3
    ♣ 4

After the ♣3 lead, jack, queen, and the ♠K winning, East made the strange play of the ♢A (like East did in Problem 5). Then came the ♠2. West took the spade tricks, East discarding a heart. West switched to the ♡2. South took the ♡A and lost two diamond tricks for two down, –300.

That ♢A is quite bewildering, particularly as it came from one of the world's top players. After the ♠K wins, East should simply continue with the ♠2. West takes the ♠Q, ♠A and then plays a heart. Declarer wins with the ace and plays a diamond, seven from East and . . .

To finish two down South has to finesse the ♢8. Now South might do that, but it is quite a big play. If South puts in a higher diamond, East will make three diamond tricks and take the contract three down. Playing the ♢A ensured that South would lose no more than one more diamond. Not cashing the ♢A gives the defence some chance for an extra trick.

7. Dealer North : Nil vulnerable

♠ A Q 9 8 4
♡ A 9 5
◊ K Q 5
♣ J 8

♠ K 7 6
♡ J 4 3
◊ A 7 6 2
♣ A 5 3

West	North	East	South
	1NT	2♡ (1)	2NT (2)
3♣ (3)	Pass	3♡	4♣
Pass	4♠	Pass	5♣
Double	Pass	Pass	Pass

(1) 6+ hearts or 5-5 in the black suits (2) Puppet to 3♣ (3) Pass or correct

West leads the ♡3: ace – two – eight. Declarer plays the ♣J: nine – two – ace. What should West do now?   *Solution on page 20.*

8. Dealer East : Nil vulnerable

♠ A K Q 8
♡ 7 5 4
◊ 9 4 2
♣ 9 7 4

♠ 4 3
♡ A K J 8 3
◊ A 10 7
♣ A J 2

East opens 1♡ and South overcalls 1♠. West bids 3♡ (weak, 4+ hearts), 3♠ from North. East bids 4♡, Pass : Pass to North, who bids 4♠. East doubles, all pass. West leads the ♡6: four – king – two. What would you play at trick 2? *Solution on page 21.*

9. Dealer North : East-West vulnerable

♠ Q J 9 4 2
♡ J 10 9 5 3
◇ 9 5
♣ 5

♠ 6 5 3
♡ A 2
◇ 10
♣ A 10 7 6 4 3 2

West	North	East	South
	Pass	Pass	5◇
Double	Pass	6♣	Pass
Pass	6◇	Double	All pass

West leads the ♠A: two – three – ◇3. South plays the ♣Q and West covers with the ♣K, ♣5 from dummy. What should East do?
Solution on page 22.

10. Dealer East : Both vulnerable

♠ 2
♡ J 10 5 4 2
◇ 7
♣ K Q 8 7 3 2

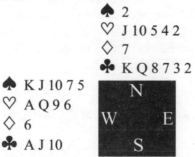

♠ K J 10 7 5
♡ A Q 9 6
◇ 6
♣ A J 10

East passes, South opens 5◇, West doubles, all pass. West leads the ◇6: seven – nine – queen. South plays the ◇A, ◇K and East follows with the ◇3, ◇2 and West discards the ♠5 and ♡6. South now plays the ♣9. Do you take the ♣A. If so, what next?
Solution on page 23.

7. From a National Teams Selection Tournament, 2014

Contract: 5♣ doubled   ♠ A Q 9 8 4
Lead: ♡3   ♡ A 9 5
                    ◇ K Q 5
                    ♣ J 8

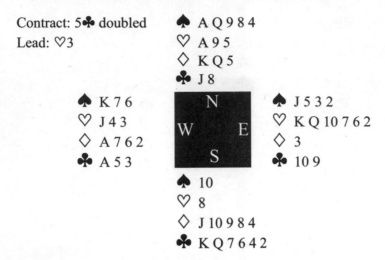

♠ K 7 6   ♠ J 5 3 2
♡ J 4 3   ♡ K Q 10 7 6 2
◇ A 7 6 2   ◇ 3
♣ A 5 3   ♣ 10 9

                    ♠ 10
                    ♡ 8
                    ◇ J 10 9 8 4
                    ♣ K Q 7 6 4 2

Given East's 3♡ bid, promising six hearts, it is clear that the defence will not score any heart tricks. The spade position also indicates that there are almost certainly no spade tricks for the defence. With only one club trick coming in, you have to hope for two diamond tricks. Take the ♣A and switch to the ◇A and a second diamond. East ruffs and the contract is one down. In practice West ducked the ♣J and took the second club. That was the end of the defence and North-South had +550.

At another table West found the defence to beat 5♣ after the ♠6 lead, but that was easier as South had bid clubs and diamonds before ending in 5♣.

Aside from sheer necessity, there was another clue for West to switch to diamonds at trick 3. East had played the ♡2 at trick 1. When a continuation of the suit led is futile, then a suit-preference signal is recommended. East intended the ♡2 as a request for diamonds since a heart continuation would be useless. Obviously West was not paying attention.

8. From the final of a National Open Teams, 2014:

Contract: 4♠ doubled
Lead: ♡6

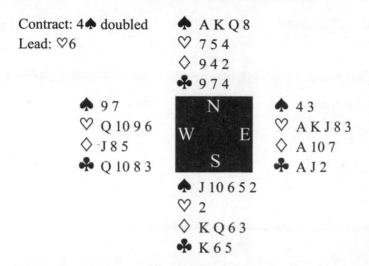

```
                    ♠ A K Q 8
                    ♡ 7 5 4
                    ◇ 9 4 2
                    ♣ 9 7 4
   ♠ 9 7                            ♠ 4 3
   ♡ Q 10 9 6                       ♡ A K J 8 3
   ◇ J 8 5                          ◇ A 10 7
   ♣ Q 10 8 3                       ♣ A J 2
                    ♠ J 10 6 5 2
                    ♡ 2
                    ◇ K Q 6 3
                    ♣ K 6 5
```

Since West has shown 4-card heart support, East knows there are no more heart tricks for the defence. East can see two tricks in the minors and all will be well if West has a minor suit king. What if South has the ♣K and ◇K? Now it might be vital to set up an extra trick in clubs or in diamonds speedily. Which one?

West has provided a strong clue with the lead of the ♡6. East knows West began with ♡Q-10-9-6. With East having five hearts, it can hardly make any difference whether West begins with the ten, the nine or the six. Since West chose the six, the lowest card, the inference is that West is indicating the lowest suit, clubs, as the location of his meagre outside strength. East should switch to a club and the defence collects two club tricks in time to beat 4♠.

At the table West actually led the ♡9. East won and returned a heart. South ruffed, crossed to ♠A, played the ◇2 to the ◇K, ♠5 to the king and the ◇4, East rose with the ace and switched to a club. Too late. South won with the ♣K and played ◇Q, ◇6, discarding a club from dummy, +590. East should switch to a minor at trick 2 anyway, but the ♡6 lead would have helped.

9. Round 19, Board 3, Bermuda Bowl (World Open Teams), 2013

Contract: 6♦ doubled   ♠ Q J 9 4 2
Lead: ♠A   ♡ J 10 9 5 3
                        ♦ 9 5
                        ♣ 5

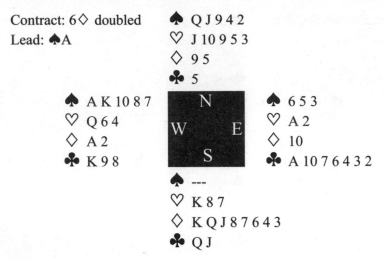

♠ A K 10 8 7   ♠ 6 5 3
♡ Q 6 4   ♡ A 2
♦ A 2   ♦ 10
♣ K 9 8   ♣ A 10 7 6 4 3 2

                       ♠ ---
                       ♡ K 8 7
                       ♦ K Q J 8 7 6 4 3
                       ♣ Q J

6♣ was due to make. North cannot come on lead to give South a spade ruff and the ♡K is onside to give East a spade discard.

A good idea for West would be to lead a trump, the ♦2, just in case East has the ♦K bare. West can cash the ♦A when in with the ♣K. As the cards lie, starting with ♦A and then the ♦2 would work just as well. The defence would come to two hearts, a diamond and two clubs for +800. That would be +13 Imps against North-South –100 in 5♦ at the other table.

When West led the ♠A, ruffed, South played the ♣Q. West covered with the ♣K and was ready to play ♦A and ♦2 when East overtook with the ♣A. He switched to diamonds, but now the defence took only four tricks, +500, +9 Imps. Overtaking was ill-judged. If West had ♦K-x, West would have ducked the ♣Q. He could afford to do so. Could South have ♣A-Q-x? Hardly. With that South would play ♣A, club, ruff, spade ruff, club ruff. In any event, East would have passed the double of 5♦ with a club suit no better than J-10-x-x-x-x.

10. Board 45, Bermuda Bowl final (World Open Teams), 2013

Contract: 5◇ doubled
Lead: ◇6

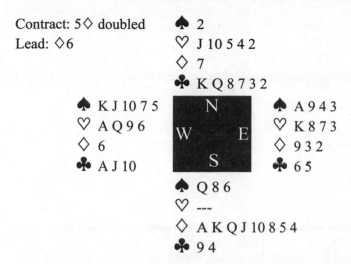

```
              ♠ 2
              ♡ J 10 5 4 2
              ◇ 7
              ♣ K Q 8 7 3 2
♠ K J 10 7 5          ♠ A 9 4 3
♡ A Q 9 6            ♡ K 8 7 3
◇ 6                 ◇ 9 3 2
♣ A J 10            ♣ 6 5
              ♠ Q 8 6
              ♡ ---
              ◇ A K Q J 10 8 5 4
              ♣ 9 4
```

At one table South opened 1◇, at the other 5◇. At both tables the contract was 5◇ doubled. Both Wests led the ◇6. South took three rounds of trumps and then played the ♣9.

If the ♣9 is a singleton, it costs a trick if you duck. If you take the ♣A and South has two or three clubs, it is vital to cash out. If you take the ♣A and play the ♡A, South makes twelve tricks.

You should have noted that East followed to the second and third diamond with the ◇3 and ◇2. Why that order and not ◇2 then ◇3? It cannot matter to East and so these idle cards can be used for other purposes. Some use it to show the length in dummy's long suit. If ◇3-then-◇2 = an even number of clubs, West should duck the first club. If you do that, as happened at one table, there are no further problems.

Others use idle cards as suit-preference. Then ◇3-then-◇2 shows interest in spades. At the other table West took the ♣A at once and switched to the ♠7 to the ace. East returned the ♠3 to show an even number. West won and cashed the ♠K, no swing.

11. Dealer South : East-West vulnerable

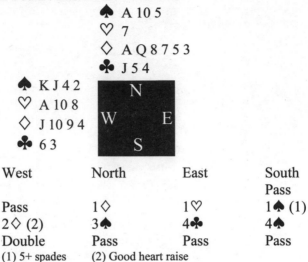

♠ A 10 5
♡ 7
◇ A Q 8 7 5 3
♣ J 5 4

♠ K J 4 2
♡ A 10 8
◇ J 10 9 4
♣ 6 3

West	North	East	South
			Pass
Pass	1◇	1♡	1♠ (1)
2◇ (2)	3♠	4♣	4♠
Double	Pass	Pass	Pass
(1) 5+ spades	(2) Good heart raise		

West leads the ♣6: four – nine – king. South plays the ◇6: jack – queen – king. East's ♣Q and ♣A win. East switches to the ♡5: nine – ten – seven. What next?   *Solution on page 26.*

12. Dealer South : Both vulnerable

♠ 10 5 2
♡ 9
◇ J 10 9 8 6 3 2
♣ 9 7

♠ J 8
♡ Q 8 7 2
◇ A Q 4
♣ Q J 8 3

W	N	E	S
			1♡
Pass	Pass	1♠	4♣
Dble	Pass	Pass	Pass

West leads the ♠J: two – nine –seven. What next?
          Solution on page 27.

13. Dealer East : East-West vulnerable

♠ Q
♡ A 10 5
♢ A Q 7 5 2
♣ A K 5 3

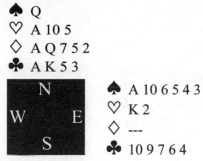

♠ A 10 6 5 4 3
♡ K 2
♢ ---
♣ 10 9 7 6 4

East opened 2♠, a weak two, Pass : Pass to North, who doubled. South showed a weak hand with 4+ hearts. North then bid 3♠, asking for a spade stopper and South bid 3NT. West doubled and everyone passed.

West leads the ♠K and continues with the ♠7 to your ace. South has followed with the ♠2 and ♠8 and discarded the ♢2 from dummy. What do you play at trick 3?

Solution on page 28.

14. Dealer South : East-West vulnerable

♠ 8 4
♡ 7 5 4 2
♢ K Q 10 4 2
♣ Q 8

♠ K J 7 5 2
♡ K J 10
♢ J 9 6
♣ 5 4

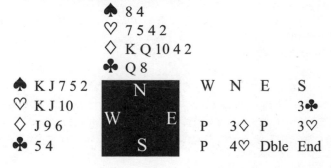

W	N	E	S
			3♣
P	3♢	P	3♡
P	4♡	Dble	End

West leads the ♠2: four – ace – ten and East returns the ♠3: queen – king – eight. How would you continue at trick 3?

Solution on page 29.

11. Round 3, Board 2, Rosenblum (World Open Teams), 2010

Contract: 4♠ doubled
Lead: ♣6

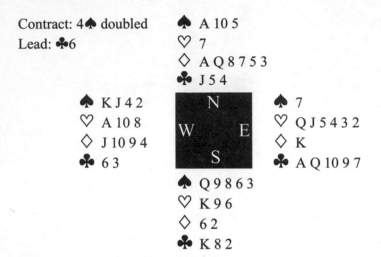

♠ A 10 5
♡ 7
◇ A Q 8 7 5 3
♣ J 5 4

♠ K J 4 2
♡ A 10 8
◇ J 10 9 4
♣ 6 3

♠ 7
♡ Q J 5 4 3 2
◇ K
♣ A Q 10 9 7

♠ Q 9 8 6 3
♡ K 9 6
◇ 6 2
♣ K 8 2

After East won with the ◇K and cashed the ♣Q, ♣A, East correctly switched to a low heart. If East switches to a top heart, South ducks and West would almost certainly do so, too. East wanted West on lead for the diamond ruff. When West won with the ♡10, West should have played a diamond. The clue was in East's carding in clubs: ♣Q, then the ♣A. Lower club, then high club = suit-preference for the lower suit. With no interest in diamonds, East would have played ♣A, then the ♣Q before switching to hearts.

As East-West can make 4♡, it is important to collect as much as possible from 4♠ doubled. If West plays a diamond at trick 6, East ruffs and reverts to hearts. When dummy ruffs, West is assured of two trump tricks and the defenders come to seven tricks for +800.

At the table West played the ♡A at trick 6. Declarer ruffed and could now escape for –500 by playing ♠A, then ◇A and another diamond, ruffing low and playing the ♡K. West comes to two spade tricks, but declarer has seven tricks.

12. From the final of a national team selection, 2011

Contract: 4♣ doubled
Lead: ♠J

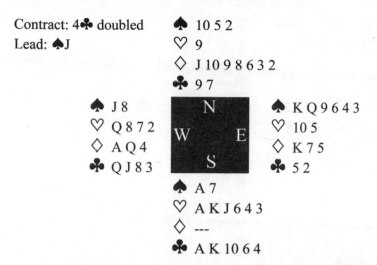

♠ 10 5 2
♡ 9
◇ J 10 9 8 6 3 2
♣ 9 7

♠ J 8
♡ Q 8 7 2
◇ A Q 4
♣ Q J 8 3

♠ K Q 9 6 4 3
♡ 10 5
◇ K 7 5
♣ 5 2

♠ A 7
♡ A K J 6 4 3
◇ ---
♣ A K 10 6 4

What is the spade position? With ♠A-K East would have won trick 1. If East's spades are headed by A-Q, South would have won trick 1. With ♠A-K-Q East should have overtaken the ♠J and switched to a trump. West can deduce that South has the ♠A and East the ♠K-Q.

West should continue with the ♠8. South can win and play ♡A, ♡K, heart ruff, diamond ruff, heart ruff. The hearts are set up, but after ruffing the next card from dummy, South loses trump control. South has ♡J-6, ♣A-K-10 and the defence can hold South to just the top trumps, no matter how declarer plays.

As it happens, switching to the ♣Q works on the actual layout, but if South had ♡A-K-J-10-x-x, South could make ten tricks if West switches to a top trump.

At the table West switched to the ◇A at trick 2. That was fatal, as it allowed South to score the three low trumps. After diamond ruff, South played ♡A, heart ruff, diamond ruff, heart ruff, diamond ruff, ♣A, ♣K, ♠A, ♡K for ten tricks and +710.

13. From the qualifying rounds of a national open teams, 2011

Contract: 3NT doubled
Lead: ♠K, then ♠7

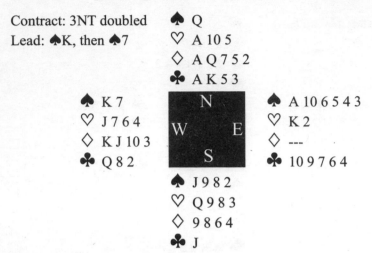

♠ Q
♡ A 10 5
◇ A Q 7 5 2
♣ A K 5 3

♠ K 7
♡ J 7 6 4
◇ K J 10 3
♣ Q 8 2

♠ A 10 6 5 4 3
♡ K 2
◇ ---
♣ 10 9 7 6 4

♠ J 9 8 2
♡ Q 9 8 3
◇ 9 8 6 4
♣ J

West's ♠K lead and ♠7 at trick 2 makes it clear that South began with ♠J-9-8-2. Playing another spade is futile. It gives South an extra spade trick and you lack the entries to establish the spades and to cash spade winners.

At the table East switched to the ♡K, even though South was known to have four hearts. Dummy's ♡A won and declarer ran the ♡10 to West's jack. West returned the ♣Q to the ♣A. South cashed two hearts and the ♠J, forcing West to pitch a club. Dummy was left with ◇A-Q-7-5, ♣K and West had ◇K-J-10-3, ♣8. South led the ◇9, ten, queen and cashed the ♣K. A low diamond to the eight end-played West, who had to give South two more tricks and the contract. South made a spade, three hearts, three diamonds and two clubs.

For the heart switch at trick 3 to be useful, West needed to have ♡Q-J-9-x. East should shift to a low club, but the ♣10 also works. That needs West to hold only ♣Q-x or ♣Q-x-x. It is easier to have a small prayer answered than a big one. Now South can make only two heart tricks and 3NT will be defeated.

14. Board 67, quarter-finals, World Women's Teams, 2013

Contract: 4♡ doubled
Lead: ♠2

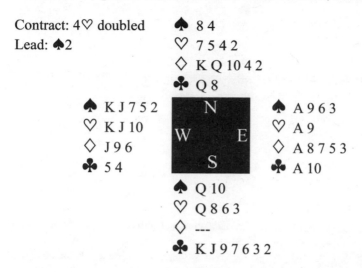

♠ 8 4
♡ 7 5 4 2
◇ K Q 10 4 2
♣ Q 8

♠ K J 7 5 2
♡ K J 10
◇ J 9 6
♣ 5 4

♠ A 9 6 3
♡ A 9
◇ A 8 7 5 3
♣ A 10

♠ Q 10
♡ Q 8 6 3
◇ ---
♣ K J 9 7 6 3 2

After trick 2, you know the contract is failing. How big a penalty can you collect? South has shown up with two spades. What else? The actual 2=4=0=7 is no surprise. Could South be 2=5=0=6? Possible, but it would be strange to pre-empt with a 5-card major. Less likely is 2=4=1=6. Next West should focus on East's double. East has at most the ace in spades and the ace in diamonds. East has no indication that West has any values. It is hard to place East with anything other than the other two aces. With ♣A-K, East would have to be worried about a club void in dummy.

Best is to continue spades, but West shifted to the ◇6, king, ace, ruffed. South played the ♣2 to the queen and ace and East returned the ♣10, taken by South's king. South now played the ♡6: ten – two – nine. West was down to ♠J-7-5, ♡K-J, ◇J-9, South had ♡Q-8 and winning clubs.

A spade now would still give the defenders seven tricks for four down, +800. The ♡J or a diamond would allow South to escape for –500. When West strangely played the ♡K, South was only –300.

15. Dealer East : Nil vulnerable

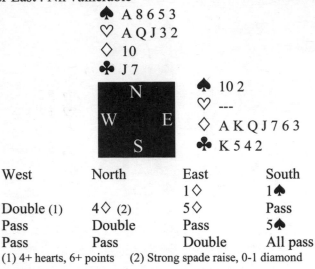

♠ A 8 6 5 3
♡ A Q J 3 2
♢ 10
♣ J 7

♠ 10 2
♡ ---
♢ A K Q J 7 6 3
♣ K 5 4 2

West	North	East	South
		1♢	1♠
Double (1)	4♢ (2)	5♢	Pass
Pass	Double	Pass	5♠
Pass	Pass	Double	All pass

(1) 4+ hearts, 6+ points   (2) Strong spade raise, 0-1 diamond

West leads the ♢9. Plan the defence for East.

Solution on page 32.

16. Dealer South : Nil vulnerable

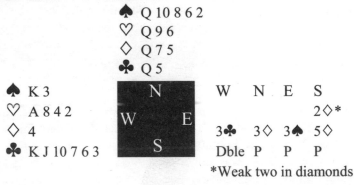

♠ Q 10 8 6 2
♡ Q 9 6
♢ Q 7 5
♣ Q 5

♠ K 3
♡ A 8 4 2
♢ 4
♣ K J 10 7 6 3

W	N	E	S
			2♢*
3♣	3♢	3♠	5♢
Dble	P	P	P

*Weak two in diamonds

West leads the ♠K: two – nine – five. What do you do next?

Solution on page 33.

17. Dealer South : Both vulnerable

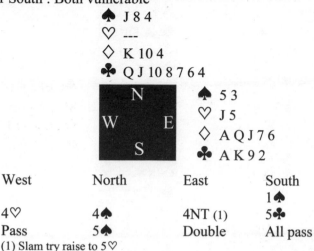

♠ J 8 4
♡ ---
♢ K 10 4
♣ Q J 10 8 7 6 4

♠ 5 3
♡ J 5
♢ A Q J 7 6
♣ A K 9 2

West	North	East	South
			1♠
4♡	4♠	4NT (1)	5♣
Pass	5♠	Double	All pass

(1) Slam try raise to 5♡

West leads the ♢8 (thirds and fifths): four – jack – two. What would you play at trick 2?

Solution on page 34.

18. Dealer North : Nil vulnerable

♠ A 2
♡ K J 8 6
♢ Q 4 3 2
♣ J 5 3

♠ J 5
♡ A 9 2
♢ A K 7 5
♣ A Q 10 8

North opens 1NT, 11-14. East doubles, South bids 2♠, West doubles, all pass. West leads the ♡3: jack – ace – four. East cashes ♢K, ♢A. West follows with the ♢J and then discards the ♣9. West ruffs East's ♢5 next and plays the ♣K and the ♣4 to East's ♣Q. What should East play now? *Solution on page 35.*

15. From a teams' match on Bridge Base Online, 2011

Contract: 5♠ doubled
Lead: ◇9

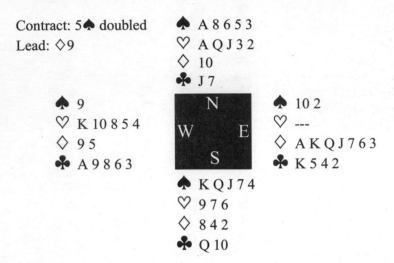

♠ A 8 6 5 3
♡ A Q J 3 2
◇ 10
♣ J 7

♠ 9
♡ K 10 8 5 4
◇ 9 5
♣ A 9 8 6 3

♠ 10 2
♡ ---
◇ A K Q J 7 6 3
♣ K 5 4 2

♠ K Q J 7 4
♡ 9 7 6
◇ 8 4 2
♣ Q 10

With the 2-2 split in clubs, East-West can make twelve tricks in either minor. At both tables the contract was 5♠ doubled and both Wests led the ◇9. One East won with the ◇A, the other with the ◇J. Both Easts returned a low club, the ♣2 at one table, the ♣5 at the other table. Both Wests returned a club to East's ♣K. East reverted to a top diamond, ruffed in dummy. After ♠A, spade to the king, heart finesse, spade to the queen, heart finesse, declarer could ruff a heart and ruff the remaining diamond loser for one off.

Each East was trying to attract a heart return, but to no avail. Since you are shifting to a club at trick 2 in the hope that partner has the ace, East should play the ♣K at trick 2. When West wins the second club, West might produce a heart, since a club or a diamond is futile. The fall of South's club honours should tip West off that East did not begin with ♣K doubleton. A heart ruff takes the contract two down for +300 and +5 Imps. If West does play a third club, giving declarer a ruff-and-discard, no damage has been done as South has no losers that need to be discarded.

16. From a teams' match on Bridge Base Online, 2011

Contract: 5♦ doubled
Lead: ♠K

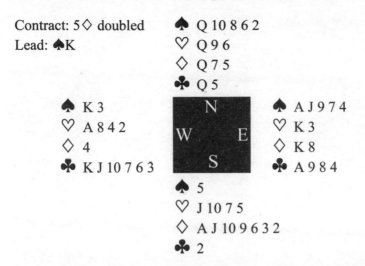

```
                    ♠ Q 10 8 6 2
                    ♡ Q 9 6
                    ♢ Q 7 5
                    ♣ Q 5
    ♠ K 3                              ♠ A J 9 7 4
    ♡ A 8 4 2          N              ♡ K 3
    ♢ 4             W     E           ♢ K 8
    ♣ K J 10 7 6 3      S             ♣ A 9 8 4
                    ♠ 5
                    ♡ J 10 7 5
                    ♢ A J 10 9 6 3 2
                    ♣ 2
```

A pre-emptive bidder is not supposed to bid twice, but when North showed diamond support, South fancied his hand with its freak shape. East-West showed that South's fancy was fanciful.

As the bidding marked East with five spades, East's spade holding was known. West took the ♠9 as suit-preference for the higher suit, hearts, and that implied the ♡K. West switched to the ♡2, away from his ace. East won and returned the ♡3. West took the ♡A and played the ♡4 for East to ruff.

East recognized that West's ♡4, his lowest heart, suit-preference, was asking for a club return. East switched to a low club, away from his ace. West won with the ♣K and returned his fourth heart. Declarer ruffed with dummy's ♢Q, but East over-ruffed.

The defenders thus notched up six tricks and +800, reasonable compensation for the hard-to-reach 6♣, which is available for East-West, who were Australian experts, David Beauchamp (West) and Ted Chadwick (East).

17. Round 4, Board 4, Rand Cup, Senior Teams, 2010

Contract: 5♠ doubled
Lead: ◇8

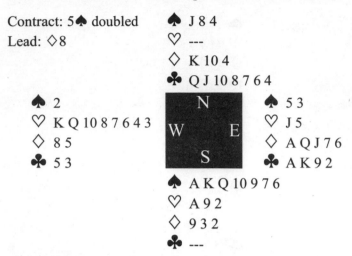

♠ J 8 4
♡ ---
◇ K 10 4
♣ Q J 10 8 7 6 4

♠ 2
♡ K Q 10 8 7 6 4 3
◇ 8 5
♣ 5 3

♠ 5 3
♡ J 5
◇ A Q J 7 6
♣ A K 9 2

♠ A K Q 10 9 7 6
♡ A 9 2
◇ 9 3 2
♣ ---

Since East-West play thirds and fifths for their opening leads (and not Middle-Up-Down), the ◇8 lead must be a singleton or a doubleton. All the diamond honours are visible. The only diamond higher than the eight is the nine, but from ◇9-8, West would lead the ◇9, and from ◇9-8-x, West would lead the low card.

After taking trick 1 with the ◇J East can defeat the contract at once via ◇A and a diamond ruff. Is there any danger in switching to a trump? After all West has the hearts and East has the minors sewn up. The danger sign for East was South's 5♣ bid. As East has the ♣A, ♣K the 5♣ cue would be based on a void.

If East gives West the diamond ruff, the contract is one down. If East switches to a trump, declarer can succeed by winning with the ♠8 in dummy and leading the ♣Q, king, ruff. (If East does not cover, South discards a diamond.) Then comes heart ruff, ♣J, ace, ruffed, heart ruff and the ♣10 allows South to discard a diamond loser and make 5♠ doubled. On the actual deal South had the ♡K and West the ♡A. East does not know that and should not take the risk that 5♠ might succeed.

18. From the final of a National Open Teams, 2011

Contract: 2♠ doubled
Lead: ♡3

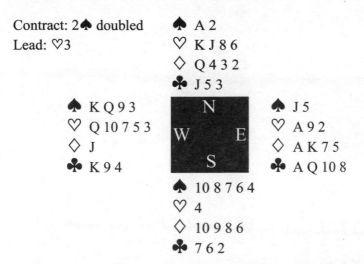

♠ A 2
♡ K J 8 6
♢ Q 4 3 2
♣ J 5 3

♠ K Q 9 3
♡ Q 10 7 5 3
♢ J
♣ K 9 4

♠ J 5
♡ A 9 2
♢ A K 7 5
♣ A Q 10 8

♠ 10 8 7 6 4
♡ 4
♢ 10 9 8 6
♣ 7 6 2

At the other table East-West had bid and made 4♡ for +420 and so East-West needed to take 2♠ doubled at least three down to collect Imps on the board. After the ♡3 lead, jack, ace, East took the ♢K, ♢A and West pitched the ♣9. East continued with the ♢5 and West ruffed. Then came the ♣K and the ♣4 to East's ♣Q. East played a fourth diamond for West to ruff. Out of clubs, West played a heart, taken by the ♡K, on which declarer discarded the club loser. Then ♠A and another spade removed the missing trumps. South was three down, East-West +500 and +2 Imps.

East can do better. West's ♣K was top from the remaining doubleton. With three clubs left, West would switch to the lowest club. After the ♣4 to the ♣Q, East should cash the ♣A and only then play the fourth diamond. That produces 800 and 9 Imps.

The defence can collect 1100, 12 Imps, if West throws a heart and not a club on the ♢A. Then diamond ruff, ♣4 to the ♣A, diamond ruff, ♣K, club to the ♣Q and the last club, ruff by West, will give East-West ten tricks!

19. Dealer West : East-West vulnerable

♠ Q J 7
♡ A Q J 6 3 2
◇ Q J 5
♣ A

♠ A 9 4
♡ 9 4
◇ A 8 6 3 2
♣ 7 4 2

West	North	East	South
1♠	Double	2♠	Pass
Pass	3♡	Pass	4♣
Pass	4♡	Pass	5♣
Pass	Pass	Double	All pass

West leads the ♠2, thirds and fifths: queen – ace – five. What would you play next as East?　　*Solution on page 38.*

20. Dealer West : Nil vulnerable

♠ 7 4
♡ K J 9 3
◇ J 9 8
♣ J 6 5 3

♠ A Q J 6 5
♡ 8 5 2
◇ 3
♣ 8 7 4 2

West opens 1♣ (any 15+ points). East bids 1◇ (any 0-7 points). South overcalls 1♠, West doubles for takeout, all pass. West leads ◇A, ◇K and ◇2. East ruffs and returns the ♣8, nine, queen. West cashes the ♣A, the ♡A and plays the ♡4. Declarer rises with the ♡K and plays dummy's ♠7. What would you play as East?
　　Solution on page 39.

21. Dealer South : East-West vulnerable

♠ 2
♡ A Q 6
◇ 8 7 4 3
♣ A K Q 8 3

♠ A K J 7 5 4
♡ J 8 5 4
◇ ---
♣ 10 6 5

West	North	East	South
			Pass
Pass	1♣	1♠	Pass
2♣ (1)	Double	2♠	3◇
Pass	5◇	Pass	Pass
Double	Pass	Pass	Pass

(1) Maximum pass with spade support

West leads the ◇A. What should East discard? West continues with the ◇K and the ◇Q. What would you discard as East?
Solution on page 40.

22. Dealer South : Both vulnerable

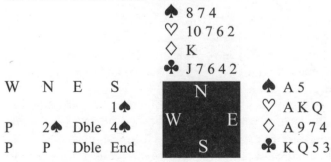

♠ 8 7 4
♡ 10 7 6 2
◇ K
♣ J 7 6 4 2

♠ A 5
♡ A K Q
◇ A 9 7 4
♣ K Q 5 3

W	N	E	S
			1♠
P	2♠	Dble	4♠
P	P	Dble	End

West leads the ◇8. Plan the defence for East.
Solution on page 41.

19. Session 5, Board 5, Generali World Women's Pairs, 2010

Contract: 5♣ doubled
Lead: ♠2

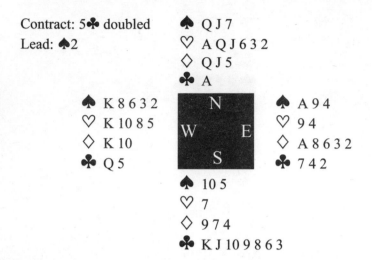

♠ Q J 7
♡ A Q J 6 3 2
◇ Q J 5
♣ A

♠ K 8 6 3 2
♡ K 10 8 5
◇ K 10
♣ Q 5

♠ A 9 4
♡ 9 4
◇ A 8 6 3 2
♣ 7 4 2

♠ 10 5
♡ 7
◇ 9 7 4
♣ K J 10 9 8 6 3

North-South were living way beyond their means. South might have passed 3♡ and North could have passed 4♣. East won the ♠2 lead, cashed the ◇A and reverted to the ♠9. West won and played the ◇K, but that was the end of the defence. East-West collected 300, which was a shared top.

You might think it is quibbling, but why settle for a shared top when you can easily score an outright top? After winning trick 1, East should switch to the ◇2, thirds and fifths. West wins and returns a diamond to the ace (or cashes the ♠K first if East is known systemically not to have four spades). East gives West a diamond ruff and the defence collects two spades, two diamonds and a ruff for +500, an absolute top.

Dummy has 17 HCP, East has 8 HCP. How can West have opened the bidding and not have the ◇K? In addition South is known to have exactly two spades (from the ♠2 lead) and is short in hearts. There is every chance that West is short in diamonds.

20. Board 54, semi-finals, World Women's Teams, 2010

Contract: 1♠ doubled
Lead: ◇A, then ◇K
then ◇2

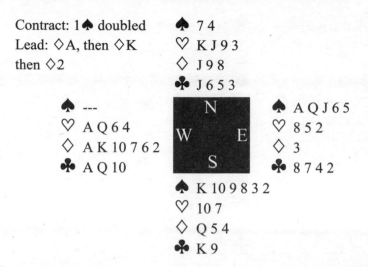

♠ 7 4
♡ K J 9 3
◇ J 9 8
♣ J 6 5 3

♠ ---
♡ A Q 6 4
◇ A K 10 7 6 2
♣ A Q 10

♠ A Q J 6 5
♡ 8 5 2
◇ 3
♣ 8 7 4 2

♠ K 10 9 8 3 2
♡ 10 7
◇ Q 5 4
♣ K 9

After two top diamonds and a diamond ruff, club to the queen, the ace of hearts and a heart, taken by the king, declarer led the ♠7. One East ducked, a little naively, and the ♠7 held the trick. East was down to ♠A-Q-J and the next spade restricted East to two more spade tricks. The defence collected two spades, one heart, two diamonds, a diamond ruff and two clubs for +300.

At another table, after the same auction and exactly the same start, East rose with the ♠A at trick 7. She reverted to a club. West won with the ♣A and played the ♡Q. East, who had thrown a heart on the second diamond, discarded a club and South ruffed.

East was down ♠Q-J-6, ♣7 and South had ♠K-10-9-8. South could play a low spade, but East won and returned a club. South ruffed and East still had a spade trick to come. The defence here collected three spades, one heart, two diamonds, a diamond ruff and two clubs for +500.

21. Board 2, quarter-finals, Rand World Seniors' Teams, 2010

Contract: 5♢ doubled
Lead: ♢A

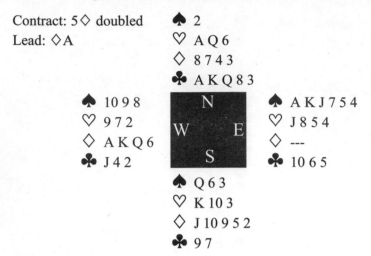

♠ 2
♡ A Q 6
♢ 8 7 4 3
♣ A K Q 8 3

♠ 1 0 9 8
♡ 9 7 2
♢ A K Q 6
♣ J 4 2

♠ A K J 7 5 4
♡ J 8 5 4
♢ ---
♣ 10 6 5

♠ Q 6 3
♡ K 10 3
♢ J 10 9 5 2
♣ 9 7

North's raise to 5♢ reveals a very optimistic view of life. The value action on the North cards is to pass 3♢ or at the very most raise to 4♢. West was happy with the development and expressed this delight with a double.

West began with the top diamonds. East signalled encouragingly in spades, but West persisted with a fourth diamond. This was not a good idea as the club suit looked to give declarer five tricks and if South had the ♡K, quite likely for the 3♢ bid with no top cards in either minor, declarer would have ten tricks. Declarer discarded the spade losers and went only one down.

Still, East might have been more helpful and more adamant in discarding. East knows the defence can come to only one spade trick. The ♣10 as first discard lets West know that the clubs are running and simultaneously asks for a spade switch (high card = high suit). The second discard should be the ♠A and the third a discouraging card in hearts. Now the defence should collect four tricks, although West should have led a spade at trick 4 anyway.

22. From a National Open Teams, 2014

Contract: 4♠ doubled
Lead: ◇8

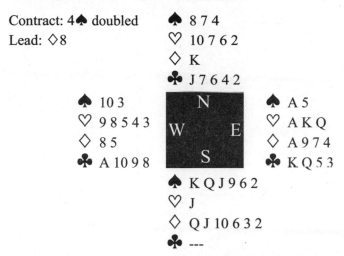

♠ 874
♡ 10 7 6 2
◇ K
♣ J 7 6 4 2

♠ 10 3
♡ 9 8 5 4 3
◇ 8 5
♣ A 10 9 8

♠ A 5
♡ A K Q
◇ A 9 7 4
♣ K Q 5 3

♠ K Q J 9 6 2
♡ J
◇ Q J 10 6 3 2
♣ ---

As always, your first job is to count dummy's points and your own. You have 22, dummy has four. That leaves South with at most 14 points. How could South jump to game with 14 points opposite an expected 6-9. South must therefore have extreme shape.

Next, focus on the opening lead. Here it is the huge clue to beating the contract. The ◇8 can be a singleton or a doubleton (not M.U.D., as you have the ◇9) or from ◇Q-10-8. Why would partner choose a risky diamond lead when a safe heart lead was available. If you reject the ◇Q-10-8 holding, then partner has two diamonds and hence South has six. That means South has a 6-6 pattern or perhaps 5-6. East should take the ◇A and return the ◇9, take the first spade and play the ◇7. West ruffs and returns a heart in response to East's suit preference signals.

It works to play a heart at trick 2 and then revert to diamonds, but that would not be so good if South had a heart void. West did well not to lead the ♣A. Then 4♠ is unbeatable. There were 46 pairs in 4♠, of whom 42 were doubled and made, including one redoubled. Of course, not every West would have led the ◇8.

23. Dealer South : Nil vulnerable

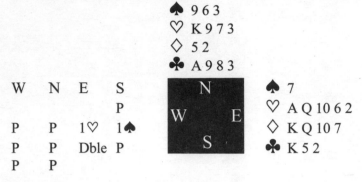

```
                  ♠ 9 6 3
                  ♡ K 9 7 3
                  ◇ 5 2
                  ♣ A 9 8 3
W   N   E   S                        ♠ 7
            P                        ♡ A Q 10 6 2
P   P   1♡  1♠                       ◇ K Q 10 7
P   P   Dble P                       ♣ K 5 2
P   P
```

West leads the ♡8: three – queen – five. East cashes the ♡A – five – ♣4 (suit-preference for diamonds) - ♡7. What next?
Solution on page 44.

24. Dealer North : Nil vulnerable

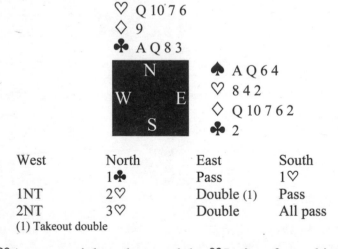

```
                  ♠ K J 8 5
                  ♡ Q 10 7 6
                  ◇ 9
                  ♣ A Q 8 3
                                     ♠ A Q 6 4
                                     ♡ 8 4 2
                                     ◇ Q 10 7 6 2
                                     ♣ 2
```

West	North	East	South
	1♣	Pass	1♡
1NT	2♡	Double (1)	Pass
2NT	3♡	Double	All pass

(1) Takeout double

Lead: ♡A – ten – eight – three and the ♡J: six – four – king. South plays ♣10: jack – queen – two and the ♠5: queen – three – seven (reverse count). What now?   *Solution on page 45.*

25. Dealer West : North-South vulnerable

♠ 8 7 4
♡ 9
♢ 10 9 8 7 5 3
♣ J 7 2

♠ 9 2
♡ A Q 8 7
♢ A K 6
♣ 9 8 6 4

West	North	East	South
2♢ (1)	Pass	2♠ (2)	Double
4♡	Pass	Pass	6♠
Pass	Pass	Double	All pass

(1) Weak two in hearts or in spades (2) Pass or correct

West leads the ♡ 2: nine – ace – four. How should East defend?
Solution on page 46.

26. Dealer West : North-South vulnerable

♠ K 7
♡ 10 9 6
♢ K J 10 6 2
♣ J 10 5

♠ 8 4
♡ K J 7 5
♢ A 5 4 3
♣ K 8 3

W	N	E	S
P	P	1♣	3♠
Dble	4♠	P	P
Dble	P	P	P

West leads the ♠8: seven – queen – ace. South plays the ♢Q. How would you defend as West?
Solution on page 47.

23. From a teams' match on BBO, 2014

Contract: 1♠ doubled
Lead: ♡8

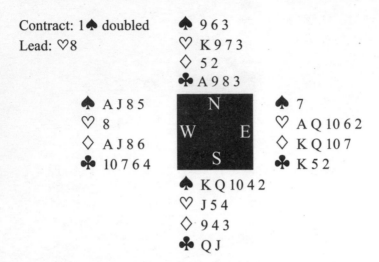

♠ 9 6 3
♡ K 9 7 3
♢ 5 2
♣ A 9 8 3

♠ A J 8 5
♡ 8
♢ A J 8 6
♣ 10 7 6 4

♠ 7
♡ A Q 10 6 2
♢ K Q 10 7
♣ K 5 2

♠ K Q 10 4 2
♡ J 5 4
♢ 9 4 3
♣ Q J

East won trick 1 with the ♡Q and cashed the ♡A. At trick 3 East played the ♡10 for West to ruff. Obeying the ♡10 suit-preference signal for diamonds, West switched to the ♢A and the ♢6, won by East with the queen. East continued with a fourth heart. South discarded the ♣J and West ruffed. Declarer ruffed West's diamond exit in dummy and played a trump. West took the ♠A, but South won the next trick and drew trumps. The result was one down.

East erred by asking for a diamond return. There is no rush for the diamonds. At trick 3 East should play the ♡2 as suit-preference for clubs. West ruffs and switches to the ♣7 or ♣10 (denying interest in clubs). If South ducks, East wins and plays a fourth heart. Now the defence will come to eight tricks. South must ruff the fourth heart with the ♠10 to avoid going three down.

On the club switch it does not help declarer to rise with the ♣A and discard the ♣J on the ♡K. West ruffs with the ♠8, plays ♢A and a diamond to East. The next heart gives West two more spade tricks and declarer will be two down.

24. Board 14, Round 5, Rosenblum (World Open Teams), 2010

Contract: 3♡ doubled   ♠ K J 8 5
Lead: ♡A, then ♡J   ♡ Q 10 7 6
                      ◇ 9
                      ♣ A Q 8 3

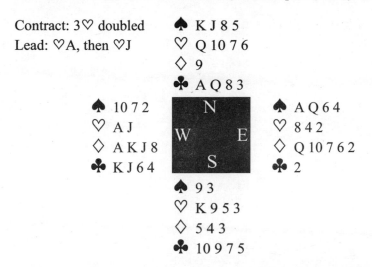

    ♠ 10 7 2   ♠ A Q 6 4
    ♡ A J   ♡ 8 4 2
    ◇ A K J 8   ◇ Q 10 7 6 2
    ♣ K J 6 4   ♣ 2

                ♠ 9 3
                ♡ K 9 5 3
                ◇ 5 4 3
                ♣ 10 9 7 5

After ♡A, ♡J won by South and the ♣10, jack, queen, South played a low spade from dummy. East took the ♠Q and played a third heart. South won with the ♡9, played the ♣7, low, low, and the ♠9, low, low, ace. The defence could take a diamond, but declarer had the rest, nine tricks, +530.

On the auction North-South were bound to have at least a 4-4 fit in hearts. West might have done better not to lead out the hearts. Maybe declarer has ♡K-Q-x-x and East has ♡10-x-x. The defence can then come to two heart tricks, but not if West leads the ♡A.

A better lead would be the ♠2, the suit partner figures to hold, given the double of 2♡. East wins the first spade and switches to the ♣2, obviously a singleton. Now when West comes in with the ♡A West returns a club. East ruffs, plays a diamond to West and receives another club ruff for two down.

As the play went, after winning with the ♠Q, East should cash the ♠A. West confirms three spades and East switches to the ◇7. When West wins, what other hope is there than a club ruff by East?

25. From the qualifying rounds of a national team selection

Contract: 6♠ doubled
Lead: ♡2

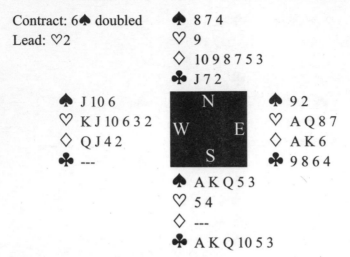

```
                    ♠ 8 7 4
                    ♡ 9
                    ◇ 10 9 8 7 5 3
                    ♣ J 7 2
♠ J 10 6                          ♠ 9 2
♡ K J 10 6 3 2                    ♡ A Q 8 7
◇ Q J 4 2                         ◇ A K 6
♣ ---                             ♣ 9 8 6 4
                    ♠ A K Q 5 3
                    ♡ 5 4
                    ◇ ---
                    ♣ A K Q 10 5 3
```

The slam that cannot be defeated is 6♣, but South chose to hide the club suit. If one plays too quickly in the East seat, one could easily do the wrong thing. You take the ♡A and promptly put the ◇A on the table. Disaster. South ruffs that, ruffs a heart in dummy, draws trumps and claims twelve tricks.

After priority #1, counting your HCP and those in dummy – not much there to count – you are no wiser. When it comes to priority #2, check the auction, you should realize that South would not jump to 6♠ with a heart loser and a diamond loser. Next, priority #3, check the opening lead and see what emerges. The opening lead is the *two* of hearts. That cannot be a genuine fourth-highest. As West began with six hearts, as indicated in the auction, it cannot be third or fifth either, if that is your agreement for length leads.

You should quickly spot that the ♡2 is a suit-preference signal for clubs and you should play the ♣4 at trick 2 as suit-preference for a diamond return. The club ruff takes 6♠ one down. If South had one diamond, the result would be three down. If you play anything but a club at trick 2, South will make the slam.

26. Round of 64, Board 19, Rosenblum (World Open Teams), 2010

Contract: 4♠ doubled
Lead: ♠8

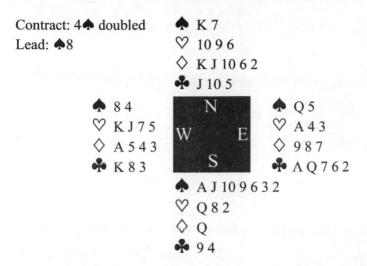

♠ K 7
♡ 10 9 6
♢ K J 10 6 2
♣ J 10 5

♠ 8 4
♡ K J 7 5
♢ A 5 4 3
♣ K 8 3

♠ Q 5
♡ A 4 3
♢ 9 8 7
♣ A Q 7 6 2

♠ A J 10 9 6 3 2
♡ Q 8 2
♢ Q
♣ 9 4

South's jump to 3♠ at unfavourable vulnerability would be a bit rich for many of us. For some, 1♠ would be quite adequate. With only one sure trick for partner, North was also living the high life.

South won the spade lead and played the ♢Q, which was allowed to win. South had no more resources apart from the trumps and so made eight tricks, –500.

If West focuses on East's 1♣ opening, West can see that that East has nothing in diamonds and only the queen in spades. Where are East's points? It is better for West to take the ♢A and watch East's signal. Since attitude is pointless and count irrelevant here (the ♠K is an entry to dummy and will draw trumps at the same time), East should give a suit-preference signal, the ♢9 to ask for a heart switch. West plays the ♡5 to the ace and East returns the ♡4. No matter which heart South plays, West can tell that East did not begin with four hearts as the ♡3 is missing. With ♡A-x-x-3 East would return the ♡3, not the ♡4. West cashes the third heart and shifts to clubs. Declarer is now three down, E-W +800.

27. Dealer West : Nil vulnerable

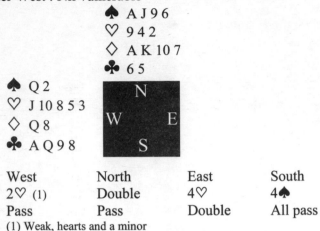

♠ A J 9 6
♡ 9 4 2
◇ A K 10 7
♣ 6 5

♠ Q 2
♡ J 10 8 5 3
◇ Q 8
♣ A Q 9 8

West	North	East	South
2♡ (1)	Double	4♡	4♠
Pass	Pass	Double	All pass

(1) Weak, hearts and a minor

West leads the ♡J: two – six – ♠3. South plays the ♠4: two – ace
– five and the ♠J: seven – eight – queen. What next?

Solution on page 50.

28. Dealer South : Both vulnerable

♠ J 6 3
♡ Q J 6
◇ K 9 7 4
♣ K 9 7

♠ 10 8
♡ K 8
◇ A J 10 5
♣ A J 6 4 3

W	N	E	S
			1♠
2♣	2♠	3♡	Dble*
4♡	4♠	P	P
Dble	P	P	P

*Game invitation in spades

West leads the ♡K: six – nine – ten. E-W play low-encouraging.
What would you play at trick 2?

Solution on page 51.

29. Dealer East : East-West vulnerable

    ♠ K Q 8
    ♡ 10 9 8 4
    ◇ K 3
    ♣ 8 7 5 4

    ♠ ---
    ♡ K Q 5 3 2
    ◇ 10 9 8 7 5
    ♣ 10 9 6

West	North	East	South
		Pass	1♠
Pass	2♠	Pass	3♠
Pass	4♠	Pass	Pass
Double	Pass	Pass	Pass

West leads the ◇A, followed by the ◇6. Which diamonds would
you play as East?

Solution on page 52.

30. Dealer West : Both vulnerable

    ♠ Q 2
    ♡ 10 6
    ◇ A K Q J 6 3
    ♣ K 7 5

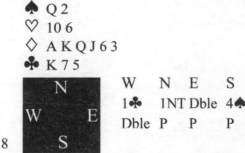

    ♠ K 3
    ♡ K J 7
    ◇ 10 2
    ♣ A Q J 10 9 8

W	N	E	S
1♣	1NT	Dble	4♠
Dble	P	P	P

West leads the ◇10: ace – nine – four. Declarer plays the ◇K:
eight – ♡3 – ◇2, followed by the ◇Q: five – ♡5 – ♠3.
What would you do now as West?

Solution on page 53.

27. From the qualifying rounds of a national team selection, 2014

Contract: 4♠ doubled
Lead: ♡J

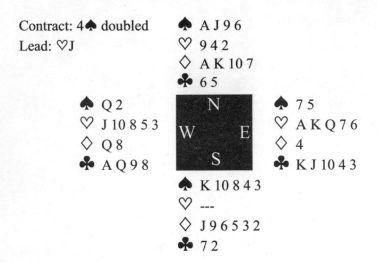

The basis of East's double of 4♠ is a mystery. East knows there is at most one heart trick for the defence, perhaps none. East has potential for a club trick, but no certainty. East is hoping for two or more defensive tricks from West. That is a lot to expect from a weak opener, even though West has no values in hearts.

Maybe East was hoping for a diamond lead and a diamond ruff later. It was lucky for East-West that West did not lead a diamond. That would give South thirteen tricks if South picks up the ♠Q.

One thing East's double did achieve. It caused declarer to mispick the spades. On trick 1 East played the ♡6, the lowest card as suit-preference for clubs. In trumps East played ♠5, then ♠7. Although lowest first is normal from two trumps, East's play in trumps does not indicate a desire for anything other than clubs. West was oblivious to all this and switched to the ◇Q at trick 4 and declarer made twelve tricks. If West considers the basis for East's double, skimpy though it is, West should realise that, with nothing useful in diamonds, East must have the ♣K. You might as well hold declarer to ten tricks.

28. Board 36, final, Rosenblum (World Open Teams), 2010

Contract: 4♠ doubled
Lead: ♡K

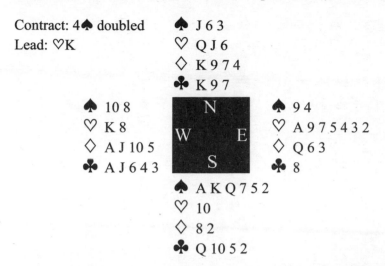

♠ J 6 3
♡ Q J 6
◇ K 9 7 4
♣ K 9 7

♠ 10 8
♡ K 8
◇ A J 10 5
♣ A J 6 4 3

♠ 9 4
♡ A 9 7 5 4 3 2
◇ Q 6 3
♣ 8

♠ A K Q 7 5 2
♡ 10
◇ 8 2
♣ Q 10 5 2

The contract was 4♠ at both tables. At the other table it went:

West	North	East	South
			1♠
2♣	2♠	Pass	3♣ (1)
Pass	4♠	Double	All pass

(1) Long suit trial bid

Here West led the ♣A and continued with the suit-preference ♣3. East returned a diamond to the ace and received another club ruff. East cashed the ♡A for two down, East-West +500. After the problem auction and East's discouraging ♡9, West played the ♣A, followed by the ♣3. East also scored two ruffs, no swing.

West can see eight clubs and eight diamonds. Is there a clue why West should switch to clubs rather than diamonds? When dummy turns up with a menacing holding, like the Q-J-6 here, when a continuation is not primarily attractive, one could play that the extreme cards are suit-preference, ♡9 (diamonds) or ♡2 (clubs), and a middling card asks for the suit led to be continued.

29. From a teams' match on BBO (Bridge Base Online)

Contract: 4♠ doubled
Lead: ◇A, then ◇6

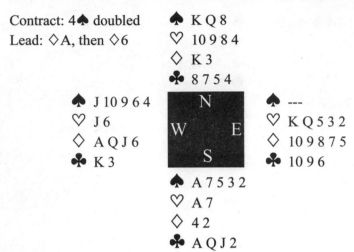

♠ K Q 8
♡ 10 9 8 4
◇ K 3
♣ 8 7 5 4

♠ J 10 9 6 4
♡ J 6
◇ A Q J 6
♣ K 3

♠ ---
♡ K Q 5 3 2
◇ 10 9 8 7 5
♣ 10 9 6

♠ A 7 5 3 2
♡ A 7
◇ 4 2
♣ A Q J 2

With 15 HCP, two doubletons and a 6-loser hand, South had just enough to justify a game try. With no convenient long suit trial or short suit trial, South invited with 3♠ and North was certainly entitled to accept. Had the spades been 3-2, 4♠ would have made.

On the ◇A, East played the ◇10. Since there is little point in continuing diamonds, East's card should not be attitude or count, but suit-preference. That is what East intended. Not keen to open a new suit, West continued with the ◇6 and East played the ◇5. South played a club to the queen and king. West played a third diamond, ruffed with the ♠8, and South discarded the ♡7. Declarer had to lose two spades and that was one down, −100.

Why did West go wrong? West took East's ◇5 as a count card in diamonds. As the ◇2, ◇3, ◇4 had all appeared, West read the ◇5 as showing an original holding of four diamonds and so the third diamond could not cost. To avoid this loss, East should play the ◇10 on the first diamond and the ◇9 on the second diamond. This might help to reinforce the suit-preference message.

30. Board 7, final, NEC Cup Japan), 2013

Contract: 4♠ doubled
Lead: ◇10

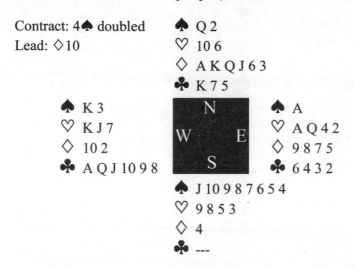

♠ Q 2
♡ 10 6
◇ A K Q J 6 3
♣ K 7 5

♠ K 3
♡ K J 7
◇ 10 2
♣ A Q J 10 9 8

♠ A
♡ A Q 4 2
◇ 9 8 7 5
♣ 6 4 3 2

♠ J 10 9 8 7 6 5 4
♡ 9 8 5 3
◇ 4
♣ ---

After declarer discarded two low hearts on the diamonds, West ruffed the third round and switched to the ♣A. South ruffed and played a trump. East won and the defenders collected two hearts for one down and +200.

Did you notice East's carding on the first two tricks? East played the ◇9 and then the ◇8. What did that mean?

If you read that diamond play as suit-preference, then East is asking for a heart shift. West might have concentrated on East's double of 1NT. East has nothing in diamonds or in clubs. Where are East's values for the double? East must have the ♡A and the ♠A. The ♡A-Q and the ♠J would not be enough to double 1NT.

West might have done better by playing the ♡7 at trick 4. East wins with the ♡A and as the ♡5 and ♡3 have appeared, the ♡7 is West's lowest, showing interest in hearts. If East plays the ♡Q next and then another diamond, the result is two down, +500. If East switches to clubs after the ♡A, West will win the *post mortem*.

31. Dealer North : North-South vulnerable

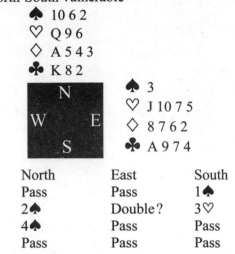

```
            ♠ 10 6 2
            ♡ Q 9 6
            ◇ A 5 4 3
            ♣ K 8 2
                            ♠ 3
                            ♡ J 10 7 5
                            ◇ 8 7 6 2
                            ♣ A 9 7 4
```

West	North	East	South
	Pass	Pass	1♠
Pass	2♠	Double?	3♡
Pass	4♠	Pass	Pass
Double	Pass	Pass	Pass

West leads the ♣5, two from dummy. How should East defend?
         Solution on page 56.

32. Dealer West : North-South vulnerable

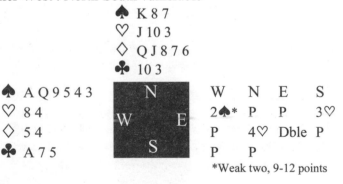

```
            ♠ K 8 7
            ♡ J 10 3
            ◇ Q J 8 7 6
            ♣ 10 3
♠ A Q 9 5 4 3
♡ 8 4
◇ 5 4
♣ A 7 5
```

W	N	E	S
2♠*	P	P	3♡
P	4♡	Dble	P
P	P		

*Weak two, 9-12 points

What would you lead as West? In practice West led the ◇5: queen
– ace – two. East switched to the ♠J, two from South . . .
Plan West's defence.
         Solution on page 57.

33. Dealer South : Both vulnerable

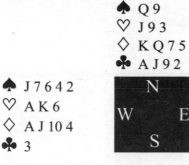

                    ♠ Q 9
                    ♡ J 9 3
                    ◇ K Q 7 5
                    ♣ A J 9 2

♠ J 7 6 4 2
♡ A K 6
◇ A J 10 4
♣ 3

West	North	East	South
			Pass
1♠	Pass	3♠ (1)	4♡
Pass	Pass	Double	All pass

(1) Pre-emptive raise, 4+ spades 0-6 points

West leads the ♣3: two – king – queen. East switches to the ♠3:
ace – six – nine. South plays the ◇6: ace – five – nine. What
should West do now?

Solution on page 58.

34. Dealer North : North-South vulnerable

                    ♠ J 10 7 2
                    ♡ J 10 5
                    ◇ A K Q 6
                    ♣ Q J

W	N	E	S
	1♣	1♠	2♡*
P	P	3♣	P
P	3♡	Dble	End

                                        ♠ A K 9 8 5
                                        ♡ ---
                                        ◇ 10 9
                                        ♣ A K 9 5 3 2

*Not forcing

West leads the ♠Q, followed by the ♠6: ten – king – four.
How would you continue as East?

Solution on page 59.

31. From a qualifying round for a National Open Teams, 2014

Contract: 4♠ doubled
Lead: ♣5

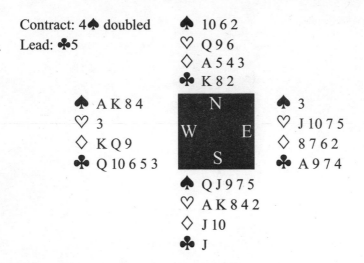

♠ 10 6 2
♥ Q 9 6
◇ A 5 4 3
♣ K 8 2

♠ A K 8 4
♥ 3
◇ K Q 9
♣ Q 10 6 5 3

♠ 3
♥ J 10 7 5
◇ 8 7 6 2
♣ A 9 7 4

♠ Q J 9 7 5
♥ A K 8 4 2
◇ J 10
♣ J

East is at least an ace short for a takeout double by a passed hand, even allowing for the favourable vulnerability. This kind of action will often mislead partner. The sound action for East is to pass.

Still, all would have been well if the defence had not stumbled. A good lead for West would have been the ♥3. Later West can put East in via the ♣A and receive a heart ruff. With a strong 4-card holding in trumps, West preferred to try for a forcing defence and led the ♣5. When dummy played low, East should have played the ♣A. A club return or a diamond switch would defeat 4♠.

When East played the ♣7, South won and led the ♠J: four – two – three and the ♠5, taken by the ♠K. East discarded a diamond. A club now would still defeat 4♠, but West assumed South had the ♣A. West switched to the ◇K, taken by the ace. The ♠10 went to West and, figuring that East had to have the ♥A for the takeout double, West tried the ♥3: nine – ten – ace. South drew West's trump, crossed to the ♥Q, picked up East's heart holding and made ten tricks, +790.

32. Round 17, Board 2, D'Orsi World Seniors Teams, 2014:

Contract: 4♡ doubled
Lead: ◇5

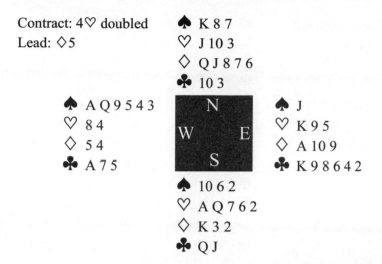

```
                    ♠ K 8 7
                    ♡ J 10 3
                    ◇ Q J 8 7 6
                    ♣ 10 3
♠ A Q 9 5 4 3              ♠ J
♡ 8 4                     ♡ K 9 5
◇ 5 4                     ◇ A 10 9
♣ A 7 5                   ♣ K 9 8 6 4 2
                    ♠ 10 6 2
                    ♡ A Q 7 6 2
                    ◇ K 3 2
                    ♣ Q J
```

West should have sought the basis for East's double of 4♡. East was not strong enough to bid after West's semi-constructive 2♠, but was good enough to double 4♡. East cannot have a trump stack. North-South should have eight or more trumps combined and so East has at most three trumps. It should not be hard to deduce that East is short in spades and is hoping for spade ruffs.

West should lead ♠A, followed by the suit-preference ♠3. East ruffs, returns a club to West's ace and receives another spade ruff. East cashes the ♣K and the ◇A and South is three off, E-W +800!

In practice West began with the ◇5, queen, ace. No damage done, the defence can still collect the same tricks: ♠J to the ace, ♠3 ruffed, club to the ace, spade ruff, ♣K, +800. It did not quite pan out that way. After ◇5 to the ace, the ♠J came back, but West had a senior moment and ducked. It is enough to make a grown man weep. South drew trumps via a couple of finesses and made five hearts, four diamonds and a spade, +790.

33. Semi-final, Round 1, Board 7, World Mixed Teams, 2014

Contract: 4♡ doubled
Lead: ♣3

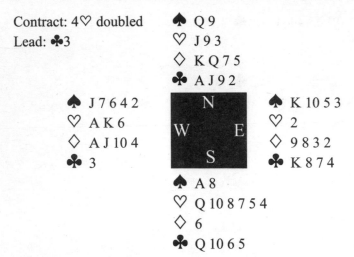

    ♠ Q 9
    ♡ J 9 3
    ◇ K Q 7 5
    ♣ A J 9 2

♠ J 7 6 4 2   ♠ K 10 5 3
♡ A K 6   ♡ 2
◇ A J 10 4   ◇ 9 8 3 2
♣ 3   ♣ K 8 7 4

    ♠ A 8
    ♡ Q 10 8 7 5 4
    ◇ 6
    ♣ Q 10 6 5

After West led the singleton club, declarer ducked in dummy and East won with the ♣K. South's ♣Q convinced East that West had led the ♣3 from 10-6-5-3 and so East switched to the ♠3. Had South ducked that, he could have escaped for one down, but because of East's pre-emptive raise, South placed the ♠K with West and rose with the ♠A. When he led the ◇6, West took the ◇A and played the *two* of spades. East won and switched to the ♡2. The defence could now take only five tricks for +500.

The ♠2 was intended as a suit-preference signal for clubs. As South had shown up with the ♠A West's lead of the ♣3, rather than a normal spade, was now likely to be a singleton. However, East did not find the club return.

West could help East by cashing the ♡A, ♡K and then playing the ♠2. Now since a diamond or a spade return is futile, East has no reason to play anything but a club back. That gives West a club ruff and 4♡ doubled would be three down, E-W +800. This is the sort of defence that you can find in Hugh Kelsey's excellent book, *Killing Defence At Bridge*.

34. Round 14, Board 6, Polish Premier League, 2015

Contract: 3♥ doubled
Lead: ♠Q

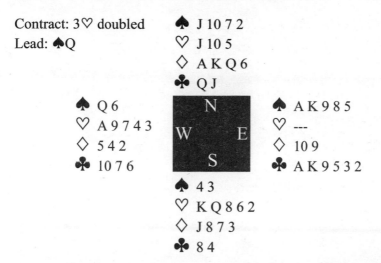

Negative free bids such as South's 2♥ are not generally popular. If the South hand is good enough for 2♥, then North should not be competing to the three-level with a minimum, balanced opening. At teams it is often wrong to bid three over three and here it cost North-South plenty to what end? To prevent a 3♣ part-score?

After winning the second spade, it is tempting for East to play a third spade for West to ruff or over-ruff South. Whether East plays a low spade or the ♠A at trick 3, South can escape for two down and give East-West 500. That would be +2 Imps, as East-West at the other table scored 420 in 5♣.

West, Krzysztof Jassem, and East, Martin Mazurkiewicz, winners of the 2014 Rosenblum (World Open Teams) made no mistake. After the ♠K, East cashed ♣K, ♣A and only then played the ♠A. South ruffed high and West discarded a diamond. After ♥2, seven, ten, South played diamonds. West ruffed the third round and played ♥A and a heart to dummy's jack. The next card from dummy allowed West to score the ♥9 for three down, +800, +9 Imps. Had North passed 3♣, he would have been +6/7 Imps instead of –9.

35. Dealer South : East-West vulnerable

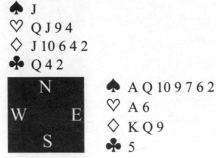

♠ J
♥ Q J 9 4
♦ J 10 6 4 2
♣ Q 4 2

♠ A Q 10 9 7 6 2
♥ A 6
♦ K Q 9
♣ 5

West	North	East	South
			Pass
Pass	Pass	1♠	3♣
4♣ (1)	5♣	6♠	7♣
Double	Pass	Pass	Pass

(1) Strong spade raise

After ♦A: two – nine –three, West switches to the ♠8: jack – ace
– ♣6. South cashes ♣A, ♣K (♣7, ♣8 from West) and plays the
♦8: seven – four – queen. What now?   *Solution on page 62.*

36. Dealer West : North-South vulnerable

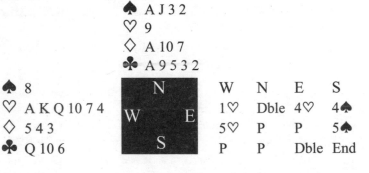

♠ A J 3 2
♥ 9
♦ A 10 7
♣ A 9 5 3 2

♠ 8
♥ A K Q 10 7 4
♦ 5 4 3
♣ Q 10 6

W	N	E	S
1♥	Dble	4♥	4♠
5♥	P	P	5♠
P	P	Dble	End

West leads the ♥A: nine – two – six. What do you play next?
        Solution on page 63.

37. Dealer West : Both vulnerable

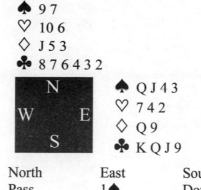

♠ 9 7
♡ 10 6
◇ J 5 3
♣ 8 7 6 4 3 2

♠ Q J 4 3
♡ 7 4 2
◇ Q 9
♣ K Q J 9

West	North	East	South
1♣	Pass	1♠	Double
Redouble	2♣	Double	4♡
Double	Pass	Pass	Pass

West leads the ♡A: six – two – five and switches to the ♣5: two – jack – ♡5. South plays ◇A, ◇K and the ◇7 to the ◇J. East ruffs. What next?

Solution on page 64.

38. Dealer North : East-West vulnerable

♠ 9 6 3
♡ A K 9 8 3
◇ A Q 5
♣ Q 7

♠ ---
♡ 6 5
◇ J 7 6 3
♣ A K J 9 8 3 2

W	N	E	S
	1♡	3♣	3♠
3NT	4♠	P	P
Dble	P	P	P

West leads the ♣4: seven – jack – six. How would you continue with the East cards?

Solution on page 65.

35. From a BBO match between Australia and Singapore, 2011

Contract: 7♣ doubled
Lead: ◇A, then ♠8

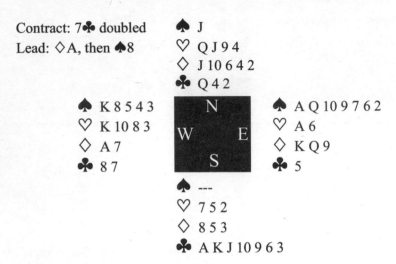

```
                    ♠ J
                    ♡ Q J 9 4
                    ◇ J 10 6 4 2
                    ♣ Q 4 2
♠ K 8 5 4 3                        ♠ A Q 10 9 7 6 2
♡ K 10 8 3                         ♡ A 6
◇ A 7                              ◇ K Q 9
♣ 8 7                             ♣ 5
                    ♠ ---
                    ♡ 7 5 2
                    ◇ 8 5 3
                    ♣ A K J 10 9 6 3
```

South's pass as dealer at favourable vulnerability was surprising. A 4♣ or even 5♣ opening looks sensible. At the other table South opened 2♣ (5+ clubs, 10-14 points). There East-West also reached the unbeatable 6♠ and South sacrificed in 7♣ doubled, too. The Singapore East-West collected their five top tricks for +1100. If the defence can find the heart ruff early, they could score 1400.

After the auction in the problem West led the ◇A. As East-West played reverse attitude, East's ◇9 looked like a discouraging signal to West. He switched to the ♠8, suit-preference for hearts. South ruffed, drew trumps and led the ◇8: seven – four – queen. East could not be sure who held the last diamond and switched to the ♡A, then ♡6. West won, but was end-played. Whether he played a heart or a spade for a ruff-and-discard, South's third diamond loser vanished. East-West +800 and –7 Imps.

It is reasonable for East not to play the third diamond just in case it is South that is void, but why the ♡A first? Only two heart tricks are possible and so East should switch to the ♡6. West wins and returns a heart to the ace. Now playing the ◇K cannot cost.

36. From the final of a National Seniors' Teams, 2011:

Contract: 5♠ doubled
Lead: ♡A

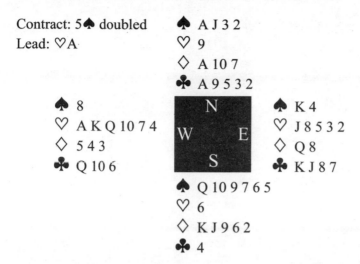

```
              ♠ A J 3 2
              ♡ 9
              ◇ A 10 7
              ♣ A 9 5 3 2
♠ 8                        ♠ K 4
♡ A K Q 10 7 4             ♡ J 8 5 3 2
◇ 5 4 3                    ◇ Q 8
♣ Q 10 6                   ♣ K J 8 7
              ♠ Q 10 9 7 6 5
              ♡ 6
              ◇ K J 9 6 2
              ♣ 4
```

Both tables had identical auctions. It was interesting that North did not double 5♡. Routine defence collects 500, better than risking a minus score in 5♠. Best defence gives North-South 800. North might lead the ♣A and South would play the ♠10 or even ♠Q, suit-preference for a diamond shift. After ◇A and a diamond to South, the ♣4 switch goes to the ace and South receives a club ruff for five tricks for the defence.

Both Wests led a top heart against 5♠ doubled and both Easts played the ♡2. Both Wests then switched to a diamond, thereby solving declarer's only significant problem. Whether you play attitude or count on partner's lead, it should be clear that neither is relevant in this situation. East's double shows values outside hearts and the ♡2 should be taken as suit-preference for clubs.

If West switches to the ♣6, South will take the ♣A and play a club, king from East, ruffed. Now, when the spade finesse loses, there is every chance, given East's jump to 4♡, that declarer will play West for the ◇Q. That will give East-West +200 instead of the −850 so richly deserved for the silly diamond switch.

37. Round 6, Board 20, Bermuda Bowl (World Open Teams), 2011

Contract: 4♡ doubled
Lead: ♡A

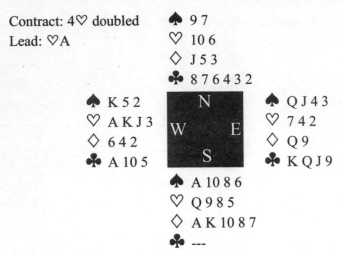

```
                    ♠ 9 7
                    ♡ 10 6
                    ◇ J 5 3
                    ♣ 8 7 6 4 3 2
   ♠ K 5 2                              ♠ Q J 4 3
   ♡ A K J 3        N                   ♡ 7 4 2
   ◇ 6 4 2      W       E               ◇ Q 9
   ♣ A 10 5         S                   ♣ K Q J 9
                    ♠ A 10 8 6
                    ♡ Q 9 8 5
                    ◇ A K 10 8 7
                    ♣ ---
```

It is comforting to us lesser bridge players to see this debacle by North-South, who were no less than members of the winning team in the 2011 Bermuda Bowl. West's redouble showed 3-card spade support and so North should have passed. He bid 2♣, intending it as a natural bid. In standard methods, if you bid an opposition suit in reply to partner's double, that shows values, normally at least game invitational. That is how South took it and jumped to game. If thoughts were lethal, North would have been in mortal danger once South saw that dummy.

West led a top heart to take a look at dummy. East played the ♡2, suit-preference for clubs, and West switched to the ♣5. South ruffed and played the top diamonds and a diamond to the jack. East ruffed and played another club. South, down to ♡Q-9, scored another ruff. The ♠A was South's last trick, down five, –1400.

You might think it churlish to chide anyone when the penalty was 1400, but the defender's credo should be, 'Every trick matters'. After ruffing the ◇J, a trump return gives E-W 1700.

38. From a National Open Teams, 2012

Contract: 4♠ doubled
Lead: ♣4

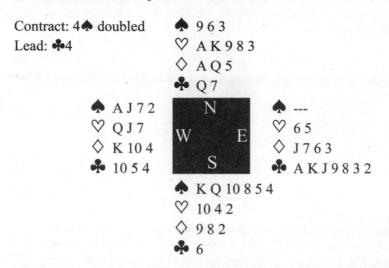

♠ 9 6 3
♡ A K 9 8 3
◇ A Q 5
♣ Q 7

♠ A J 7 2
♡ Q J 7
◇ K 10 4
♣ 10 5 4

♠ ---
♡ 6 5
◇ J 7 6 3
♣ A K J 9 8 3 2

♠ K Q 10 8 5 4
♡ 10 4 2
◇ 9 8 2
♣ 6

East won the club lead and continued with a top club. This was not fatal yet, but it was also futile. On the auction the ♣4 lead, the lowest card, was bound to be bottom from 10-5-4, not a singleton club in view of West's 3NT. With the threat of dummy's hearts providing discards for declarer, East should switch to diamonds in the hope of creating a trick there. If South has the ◇K, no damage done and if West has the ◇K, the finesse was working anyway. If East shifts to a diamond, the defence will come to two spades, a diamond and a club.

South ruffed East's club return and played the ♠K. West ducked. South played the ♡2, jack, ace, and the ♠6 went to the ♠10 and ♠J. West can switch to diamonds, but he cashed the ♠A. Now was the last chance for the defence to shift to a diamond. Dummy had ♡K-9-8-3, ◇A-Q-5. If West plays a diamond, declarer can win with the ◇Q, but has to concede a heart or a diamond. West failed the test and continued with a club, South ruffed, drew West's last trump, finessed in hearts and had ten tricks, +590.

39. Dealer North : Both vulnerable

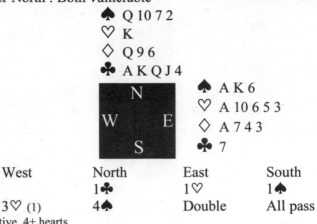

	North	East	South
West	1♣	1♡	1♠
3♡ (1)	4♠	Double	All pass

(1) Pre-emptive, 4+ hearts

West leads the ◇2: six – ace – ten. How should East continue?

Suppose you decide to switch to the ♣7: two – three – jack. South plays the ♡K from dummy: ace – seven – two (reverse count). You continue with the ◇3: jack – ♠4 - ◇9. West returns the ♣10, queen from dummy . . . How do you defend from here?

Solution on page 68.

40. Dealer East : North-South vulnerable

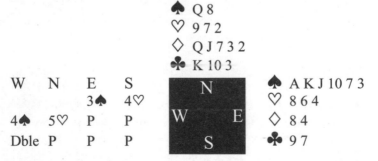

W	N	E	S
		3♠	4♡
4♠	5♡	P	P
Dble	P	P	P

West leads the ♠5, thirds and fifths: eight – ten - two. What would you play next as East?

Solution on page 69.

41. Dealer North : Nil vulnerable

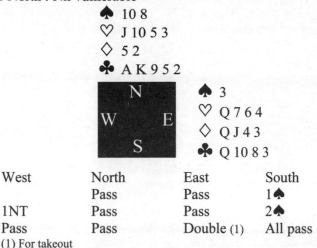

♠ 10 8
♡ J 10 5 3
◇ 5 2
♣ A K 9 5 2

♠ 3
♡ Q 7 6 4
◇ Q J 4 3
♣ Q 10 8 3

West	North	East	South
	Pass	Pass	1♠
1NT	Pass	Pass	2♠
Pass	Pass	Double (1)	All pass

(1) For takeout

West leads the ♡K: three – four (low-encourage) – two. West continues with the ♡8: five – queen – nine. What would you do now as East?

Solution on page 70.

42. Dealer East : Both vulnerable

♠ 6 5 3
♡ 9 7 3
◇ A 5 4 3
♣ Q 10 7

♠ 9 8
♡ A J 10
◇ 10 9 7 2
♣ K 9 6 2

W	N	E	S
		1◇	1♡
1NT	2♡	Dble	3♡
Dble	P	P	P

East's double of 2♡ was for takeout. West leads the ◇10: three – jack – king. South plays the ♣A: two – seven – four (reverse count) and the ♣3: king – ten – five. What now?

Solution on page 71.

39. Round 4, Board 2, Asia Pacific Open Teams, 2012

Contract: 4♠ doubled
Lead: ◇2

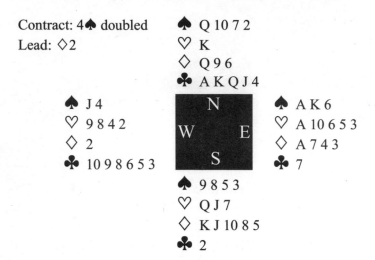

♠ Q 10 7 2
♡ K
◇ Q 9 6
♣ A K Q J 4

♠ J 4
♡ 9 8 4 2
◇ 2
♣ 10 9 8 6 5 3

♠ A K 6
♡ A 10 6 5 3
◇ A 7 4 3
♣ 7

♠ 9 8 5 3
♡ Q J 7
◇ K J 10 8 5
♣ 2

In a suit contract a defender might be reluctant to lead from an ace-high suit, even if partner has bid it or supported it. There is no such reluctance to lead a bid-and-raised suit when the holding is not headed by the ace. As East has the ♡A, why did West lead a diamond and not a heart? Self-interest rules in bridge and in many areas of life. The usual reason for not leading the partnership suit is that a singleton is more attractive. East could take the ◇A and return the ◇7 (suit-preference for hearts). West ruffs, plays a heart to the ace and receives another diamond ruff for +800.

At the table East switched to the ♣7 at trick 2. Dummy won and declarer played the ♡K. East took it and now played the ◇3. West ruffed and returned the ♣3. East ruffed with the ♠6, over-ruffed by South, who played the ♡Q to discard the ◇Q from dummy and then a spade. Result two down, East-West 500.

East should have ruffed high on the club and played a diamond for +800. East failed to count. South is known to have five diamonds (proven) three hearts from West's ♡2, reverse count, and four spades from the auction and therefore only one club.

40. From a National Open Teams, 2012

Contract: 5♡ doubled
Lead: ♠5

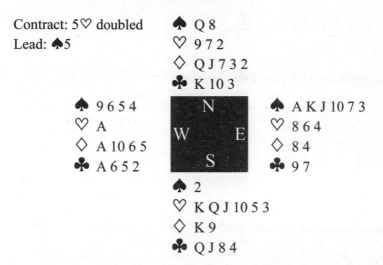

       ♠ Q 8
       ♡ 9 7 2
       ◇ Q J 7 3 2
       ♣ K 10 3

♠ 9 6 5 4   ♠ A K J 10 7 3
♡ A   ♡ 8 6 4
◇ A 10 6 5   ◇ 8 4
♣ A 6 5 2   ♣ 9 7

       ♠ 2
       ♡ K Q J 10 5 3
       ◇ K 9
       ♣ Q J 8 4

In most of the matches, the board was flat at 4♠, making five, +450, including one table in the match where the other table had the auction given in the problem. West led the ♠5. East won and attempted to cash another spade. South ruffed and played the ♡K. West took the ace, but the defence could do no better than collect West's other two aces for four tricks, +500, +2 Imps.

East could have done better. What was the rush to cash the second spade? Given West's penalty double, declarer was not about to discard a possible spade loser on any winners in dummy.

East should switch at trick 2 and the better hope to score a ruff is in clubs, dummy's shorter suit. South is more likely to be short in diamonds than in clubs. If East switches to the ♣9, West wins and returns a club. When West gains the lead with the ♡A, West gives East a club ruff. Now it is all right to try for a second spade trick. This defence will give East-West five tricks for +800 and +8 Imps. Every trick matters.

41. Round 5, Board 8, Sunchime Invitation Teams, China, 2012

Contract: 2♠ doubled
Lead: ♡K, then ♡8

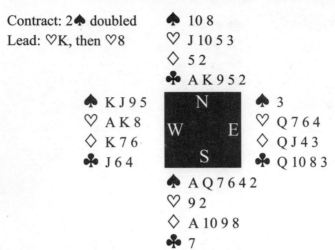

♠ 10 8
♡ J 10 5 3
♢ 5 2
♣ A K 9 5 2

♠ K J 9 5
♡ A K 8
♢ K 7 6
♣ J 6 4

♠ 3
♡ Q 7 6 4
♢ Q J 4 3
♣ Q 10 8 3

♠ A Q 7 6 4 2
♡ 9 2
♢ A 10 9 8
♣ 7

Since East had made a takeout double, West knew that East's encouraging ♡4 had to be based on the ♡Q, not a doubleton. West did well to continue with the ♡8 and East won with the ♡Q.

With the heart position known and the clubs no threat because of East's holding, one would think that the trump switch was obvious. That could eliminate the possibility of a diamond ruff. If East shifts to the ♠3 and South ducks, West wins with the jack. West can return the ♠K at once or exit with a club to the ace and play a trump later to defeat the contract.

In practice East shifted to the ♢Q at trick 3 and South ducked. Now the trump switch would be too late. South could take the ♠A, cash ♢A, ruff a diamond, ruff the ♡10, setting up the ♡J, cash the ♣A and discard two diamonds on the ♣K and the ♡J.

Anyway, that did not happen. East continued with the ♢3. South took the ♢A, cashed the ♣A, ♣K, ruffed a heart and ruffed his last diamond. Down to ♠A-Q-7-6, South played the ♠10 and let it run to West, who had to return a trump into declarer's tenace. South thus lost only five tricks and made 2♠ doubled, +470.

42. Last round, Board 7, Asia Pacific Junior Teams, 2013

Contract: 3♥ doubled
Lead: ◇10

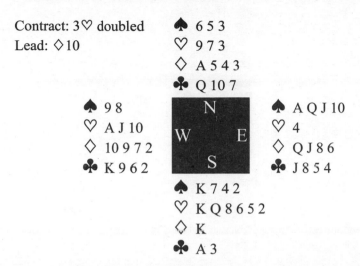

```
                    ♠ 6 5 3
                    ♡ 9 7 3
                    ◇ A 5 4 3
                    ♣ Q 10 7
      ♠ 9 8                        ♠ A Q J 10
      ♡ A J 10          N          ♡ 4
      ◇ 10 9 7 2     W     E       ◇ Q J 8 6
      ♣ K 9 6 2         S          ♣ J 8 5 4
                    ♠ K 7 4 2
                    ♡ K Q 8 6 5 2
                    ◇ K
                    ♣ A 3
```

With ten losers, a flat hand and only six points, there is not much to be said in favour of bidding 2♥ as North. If North passes and 1NT is passed out, the defence should have no trouble defeating 1NT. There was also no rush for South to bid 3♥. What will happen if South passes? West will almost certainly bid 3◇ and North-South can defeat that, too. Bidding three over three at teams is a losing policy in the long run.

After declarer played the ♣A at trick 2 and then the ♣3, taken by the king, Justin Howard, young Australian star, had to decide what to do. A minor suit allows South to restrict the spade losers to one and to make nine tricks. Rather than possibly trap East's spade honours, West played the ♡J!: three – four – queen. Declarer exited with the ♠2 to East's ♠10. East cashed the ♠A and declarer still had two trump losers. That was one down, –200.

In the other room, after the same start, West's 1NT was passed out. That was sensible action by North-South. They collected seven tricks for +100 and +7 Imps.

43. Dealer East : East-West vulnerable

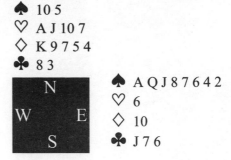

♠ 10 5
♥ A J 10 7
♦ K 9 7 5 4
♣ 8 3

♠ A Q J 8 7 6 4 2
♥ 6
♦ 10
♣ J 7 6

West	North	East	South
		4♠	Double (1)
Redouble	4NT (2)	Pass	5♣
Double	5♦	Pass	5♥
Double	Pass	Pass	Pass

(1) For takeout   (2) Two or three places to play

West leads the ♠K. Plan the defence for East.
Solution on page 74.

44. Dealer South : Both vulnerable

♠ 10 6 3 2
♥ K 7 6
♦ A 10 2
♣ 10 3 2

♠ A Q 9
♥ 10 5 2
♦ 9 6 5
♣ A K 6 5

South opened 1NT, 11-14 points, Pass : Pass : Double by East, all pass. West leads the ♣Q, ♣J and ♣4 to your ace. South follows. On the ♣K, West discards the ♥8, showing interest in spades. How would you continue as East?   *Solution on page 75.*

45. Dealer East : East-West vulnerable

♠ Q 9 5 3 2
♡ 8 3
♢ 5 3
♣ J 6 5 3

♠ K J 8 6
♡ A K Q
♢ ---
♣ A K 10 8 7 2

West	North	East	South
		1♣	3♢
Pass	4♢	Double	All pass

West leads the ♠7: two – jack – ace. South plays the ♡10: jack – three – queen. East cashes the ♠K: ten – ♣4 – ♠3. What would you play now as East.

Solution on page 76.

46. Dealer West : East-West vulnerable

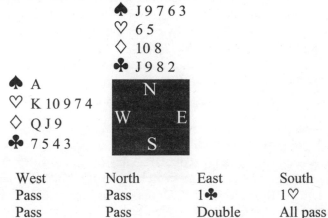

♠ J 9 7 6 3
♡ 6 5
♢ 10 8
♣ J 9 8 2

♠ A
♡ K 10 9 7 4
♢ Q J 9
♣ 7 5 4 3

West	North	East	South
Pass	Pass	1♣	1♡
Pass	Pass	Double	All pass

West leads the ♠A: three – two – four. What next?

Solution on page 77.

43. From the final of a National Open Teams

Contract: 5♡ doubled
Lead: ♠K

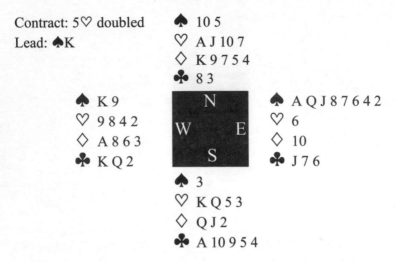

♠ 10 5
♡ A J 10 7
◇ K 9 7 5 4
♣ 8 3

♠ K 9
♡ 9 8 4 2
◇ A 8 6 3
♣ K Q 2

♠ A Q J 8 7 6 4 2
♡ 6
◇ 10
♣ J 7 6

♠ 3
♡ K Q 5 3
◇ Q J 2
♣ A 10 9 5 4

At one table East, opened 4♠ and everyone passed. There were no problems for declarer, who finished with eleven tricks for +650.

At the other table North-South competed against 4♠ and ended in 5♡ doubled, played by South. West led the ♠K. Mindful of West's double of 5♣, East overtook the ♠K and switched to the ♣7. South took the ♣A, played the ♡3 to the ♡J and returned the ◇4: ten – queen – ace. West cashed the ♣Q and reverted to the ♠9. South ruffed with the ♡K, drew trumps and had the rest of the tricks, one down, –100, but +11 Imps.

To match the other table, East-West would have needed to bid 5♠ and bidding five over five is often a losing proposition. Still, the deficit might have been reduced. After overtaking the ♠K, East would have done better by switching to the ◇10 at trick 2 and receiving a diamond ruff. Of course, that has risk attached, but East might have focussed on West's actions. West's clubs will not be headed by A-K (would have led it). Would West redouble 4♠ with only ♠K-9 and ♣A-Q-x and only some secondary values in the red suits? If you think not, then West should have the ◇A.

44. Round 22, Board 24, Asia Cup, China, 2014

Contract: 1NT doubled
Lead: ♣Q, then ♣J
and ♣4

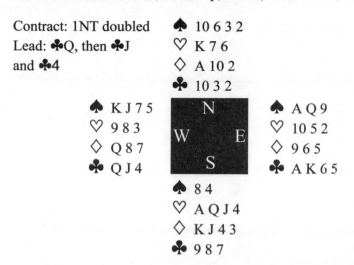

♠ 10 6 3 2
♡ K 7 6
♢ A 10 2
♣ 10 3 2

♠ K J 7 5
♡ 9 8 3
♢ Q 8 7
♣ Q J 4

♠ A Q 9
♡ 10 5 2
♢ 9 6 5
♣ A K 6 5

♠ 8 4
♡ A Q J 4
♢ K J 4 3
♣ 9 8 7

If West had led the fourth highest of his longest and strongest, East-West would have had no troubles and this problem would not have seen the light of day. After a low spade lead, East can insert the queen, cash the ace and return the nine. West collects two spades and on the fourth, East signals for a club switch. Pitching the ♡2 as suit-preference for clubs would be one way to ask for a club. Of course, you do not want to discard a club.

A diamond lead against 1NT doubled would give declarer seven tricks. A heart lead would give declarer a chance to make seven tricks, but South would probably misguess diamonds.

So much for the might-have-beens. After the ♣Q, ♣J and the ♣4, East won and cashed the fourth club. West discarded the ♡8, suit-preference for spades. East switched to the ♠A, followed by the ♠Q. As East had already shown up with A-K in clubs, East did not need much more than ♠A-Q for the double of 1NT. In case East began with ♠A-Q doubleton, West overtook the ♠Q and cashed the ♠J for one down. To save partner from erring, East should play the ♠Q at trick 5, then the ♠A and ♠9.

45. Board 48, Seniors' semi-final, Asia Pacific Teams, 2014

Contract: 4◇ doubled
Lead: ♠7

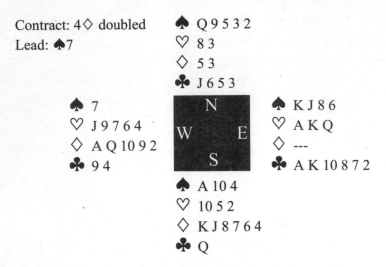

```
                    ♠ Q 9 5 3 2
                    ♡ 8 3
                    ◇ 5 3
                    ♣ J 6 5 3
  ♠ 7                              ♠ K J 8 6
  ♡ J 9 7 6 4                      ♡ A K Q
  ◇ A Q 10 9 2                     ◇ ---
  ♣ 9 4                            ♣ A K 10 8 7 2
                    ♠ A 10 4
                    ♡ 10 5 2
                    ◇ K J 8 7 6 4
                    ♣ Q
```

It is clear that 4◇ can be defeated, but by how much? This is what happened at the table: West led the ♠7: two – jack – ace. South exited with the ♡10, jack, queen. East cashed the ♠K, West discarding the ♣4, and continued with the ♠8, suit-preference for hearts. West ruffed and returned the ♡9. East won and played the ♠6. South discarded the ♣Q and West ruffed. The defence took one spade, two hearts and five diamonds, five off, E-W +1100.

That was an excellent result for East-West, but they could have done better still. East could have played the ♠6 at trick 4 as suit-preference for clubs. West ruffs and returns the ♣9 to East's ♣K. East can continue with a club or a spade or cash a heart first and then play any card. West is down to ◇A-Q-10-9 and will make four more tricks for six down, +1400.

Another option for East, after West returns a heart at trick 5, is to play the ♣A before the fourth spade. The defence then have all their outside tricks, a spade, two hearts, a club and a spade ruff with the ◇2. West cannot be prevented from winning four more tricks with the ◇A-Q-10-9, as West has convenient heart exits.

46. From the qualifying rounds of a National Open Teams, 2014

Contract: 1♡ doubled
Lead: ♠A

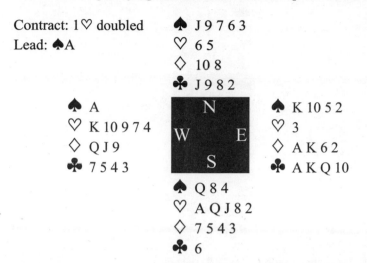

♠ J 9 7 6 3
♡ 6 5
♢ 10 8
♣ J 9 8 2

♠ A
♡ K 10 9 7 4
♢ Q J 9
♣ 7 5 4 3

♠ K 10 5 2
♡ 3
♢ A K 6 2
♣ A K Q 10

♠ Q 8 4
♡ A Q J 8 2
♢ 7 5 4 3
♣ 6

The popular spot was 3NT (25 pairs). Three tried 6NT and one made it. Two Souths played in 2♡ doubled for –1100 and –800. Six Souths were in 1♡ doubled after the auction in the problem. East-West can collect 800, but the results ranged from +800 once, through +500 (three times), +300 (twice) down to +100 (twice).

Against 1♡ doubled (or 2♡ doubled) the ♠A is a good start. It allows you to see dummy and partner's signal. East's ♠2 should be taken as a suit-preference signal for clubs. East should realise the ♠A lead is a singleton. With an easy club or diamond lead, West would not start with the ♠A from A-x, A-x-x or A-Q-x.

Recognizing the ♠2 as a request for clubs, West should switch to a club at trick 2. East wins and switches to a heart, queen (likely), king. It is important for the defence to prevent a diamond ruff and so West returns the ♡10. South wins, East discarding a spade. If South now plays the ♠Q, East wins and gives West a spade ruff. West can now switch to the ♢Q and the defence takes four diamond tricks. A club is ruffed by South, who can make a heart trick. South makes only three heart tricks. Down four.

47. Dealer West : North-South vulnerable

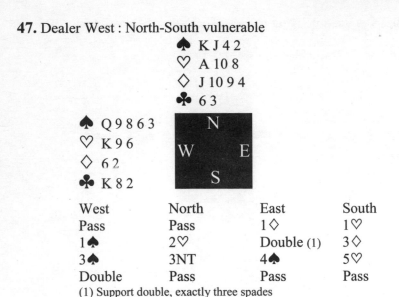

♠ K J 4 2
♡ A 10 8
◇ J 10 9 4
♣ 6 3

♠ Q 9 8 6 3
♡ K 9 6
◇ 6 2
♣ K 8 2

West	North	East	South
Pass	Pass	1◇	1♡
1♠	2♡	Double (1)	3◇
3♣	3NT	4♠	5♡
Double	Pass	Pass	Pass

(1) Support double, exactly three spades

West leads the ◇6: four – ace – king. East switches to the ♣5: queen – king – three. What now?   *Solution on page 80.*

48. Dealer West : Both vulnerable

♠ 9 4 2
♡ 9 8 6 3 2
◇ 6 4
♣ J 10 6

♠ A 8 6 3
♡ K J 5
◇ A 5 3
♣ A K 7

East opens 1♣ in third seat, South overcalls 1♠, West doubles (negative) and all pass. West leads the ♠ K: two – eight – five and switches to the ♣2: six – king – three. What would you do now?

Solution on page 81.

49. Dealer North : East-West vulnerable

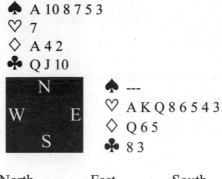

♠ A 10 8 7 5 3
♡ 7
◇ A 4 2
♣ Q J 10

♠ ---
♡ A K Q 8 6 5 4 3
◇ Q 6 5
♣ 8 3

West	North	East	South
	1♠	4♡	Pass
Pass	Double (1)	Pass	5♣
Pass	Pass	Double	All pass
(1) For takeout			

West leads the ♠K: ace – ♣3 – ♠2. What would you do now as East? Suppose you play a top heart: nine – two – seven What next?

Solution on page 82.

50. Dealer West : North-South vulnerable

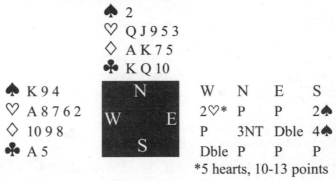

♠ 2
♡ Q J 9 5 3
◇ A K 7 5
♣ K Q 10

♠ K 9 4
♡ A 8 7 6 2
◇ 10 9 8
♣ A 5

W	N	E	S
2♡*	P	P	2♠
P	3NT	Dble	4♠
Dble	P	P	P

*5 hearts, 10-13 points

West leads the ♣A: ten – nine – six. You are playing duplicate pairs. What would you play at trick 2?

Solution on page 83.

47. Round 3, Board 2, Rosenblum (World Open Teams), 2010

Contract: 5♡ doubled
Lead: ◇6

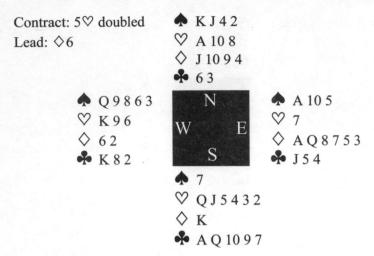

    ♠ K J 4 2
    ♡ A 10 8
    ◇ J 10 9 4
    ♣ 6 3

♠ Q 9 8 6 3   ♠ A 10 5
♡ K 9 6   ♡ 7
◇ 6 2   ◇ A Q 8 7 5 3
♣ K 8 2   ♣ J 5 4

    ♠ 7
    ♡ Q J 5 4 3 2
    ◇ K
    ♣ A Q 10 9 7

South should have passed 4♠ to North, who would have doubled for at least +500. If the deal looks familiar, it is the same one as in Problem 11, where the contract was 4♠ doubled.

A spade lead to the ace and switch to the ◇A would have put paid to 5♡, but West began with ◇6. East took the ace and switched the ♣5. This gave South a chance to make the contract by rising with the ♣A. The ♡Q comes next. If ducked, a heart to the ten is followed by the ◇J and South can eliminate the spade loser. The same applies if West covers the ♡Q. East needed to cash the ♠A at trick 2 to ensure the contract was defeated.

However, South finessed the ♣Q at trick 2 and West won. Now a spade switch is clearly right. Even if South guesses correctly, what useful discard could South have? West erred by returning a club. That gave South an easy ride to eleven tricks. After winning the club, it went ♡Q, king, ace; ◇J, queen, ruffed; ♡J and a heart to the ten. The ♠7 was discarded on the ◇10 and declarer claimed the rest. The result: East-West –850 instead of +200.

48. Board 84, quarter-finals, Bermuda Bowl, 2013

Contract: 1♠ doubled
Lead: ♠K

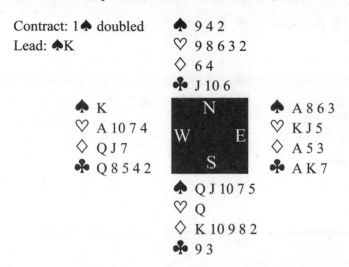

```
            ♠ 9 4 2
            ♡ 9 8 6 3 2
            ◇ 6 4
            ♣ J 10 6
♠ K                         ♠ A 8 6 3
♡ A 10 7 4      N           ♡ K J 5
◇ Q J 7      W     E        ◇ A 5 3
♣ Q 8 5 4 2     S           ♣ A K 7
            ♠ Q J 10 7 5
            ♡ Q
            ◇ K 10 9 8 2
            ♣ 9 3
```

From the ♠K lead, West's double and the ♣2 switch, East knows South began with five spades, only one heart and that West has the ♣Q. It is tempting to play ♠A and another spade to prevent diamond ruffs in dummy, but if you do, South unblocks an honour, wins the third spade in dummy and leads a diamond to the king. That gives South four tricks and East-West 800.

There is no rush for the spade play. Continuing clubs could also help South if he began with four clubs. A good idea is to force South off and the ♡K will clarify the position. That is what Andrew Robson, England, did. South discarded the ♣9 on the next heart and a diamond when West played a club to the ace. East reverted to the ♡J and South discarded another diamond.

South ruffed with the ♠10 when East switched back to the ♣7. East ducked the ♠Q, won the ♠J next with the ♠A and exited with the ♠6 to South's ♠7. South had ◇K-10-9 left and West had ♡A, ◇Q-J. South was four down, E-W +1100 and +10 Imps against −620 for 5♣ at the other table. +800 would be +5 Imps.

49. From the qualifying rounds of a national teams' event, 2011

Contract: 5♣ doubled
Lead: ♠K

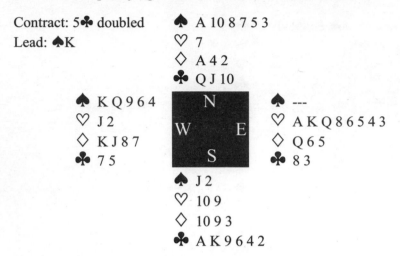

♠ A 10 8 7 5 3
♡ 7
♢ A 4 2
♣ Q J 10

♠ K Q 9 6 4
♡ J 2
♢ K J 8 7
♣ 7 5

♠ ---
♡ A K Q 8 6 5 4 3
♢ Q 6 5
♣ 8 3

♠ J 2
♡ 10 9
♢ 10 9 3
♣ A K 9 6 4 2

East-West have ten tricks in hearts without raising a sweat and so you need to collect as much as possible from 5♣ doubled. After ruffing the ♠A, it would be dramatic and brave, but successful, to play a low heart at trick 2. West wins and plays another low spade for East to ruff. Now declarer will always be three off, E-W +500.

Playing a low heart at trick 2 is unnecessary. East can cash a heart and shift to a diamond. That gives E-W five tricks and +500.

It is not good enough for East to cash a heart and switch to a club. South wins and plays the ♠J. If West wins and switches to a diamond, it is too late. Declarer takes the ♢A, ruffs a low spade, crosses to the ♣J, ruffs a low spade, ruffs the heart loser and discards two diamonds on dummy's spade winners. Now the defence collect only 100. To score 300 after ♡Q and club switch, West has to duck when South plays the ♠J. South can always make nine tricks by ducking the ♠K in dummy.

There were 27 pairs making 4♡. Nine were –500 in 4♠ doubled and two in 5♣ doubled, –100 and –300. Datum: E-W 500.

50. From the qualifying rounds of a national pairs' event, 2011

Contract: 4♠ doubled
Lead: ♣A

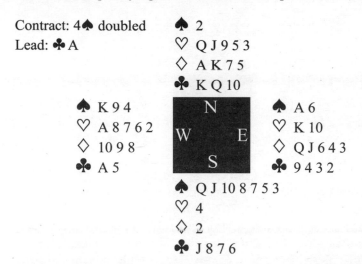

♠ 2
♡ Q J 9 5 3
◇ A K 7 5
♣ K Q 10

♠ K 9 4
♡ A 8 7 6 2
◇ 10 9 8
♣ A 5

♠ A 6
♡ K 10
◇ Q J 6 4 3
♣ 9 4 3 2

♠ Q J 10 8 7 5 3
♡ 4
◇ 2
♣ J 8 7 6

What do you make of East's ♣9? It cannot be encouraging and what would be the point of giving count here? Therefore East's ♣9 should be suit preference for the higher non-trump suit, that is, hearts. That implies that East must have the ♡K. The ♣9 also presumably denied the ♣J.

Now, focus on the double itself. Where are East's values? With nothing in clubs, East can hardly have less than the ♠A, the ♡K and something in diamonds. In that case South must be very shapely to have bid 2♠ with very few high card values.

The best defence is to switch to the ♡2 at trick 2. Without the ♡A you would switch to a high spot card in hearts. Thus, if declarer plays an honour from dummy, East knows it is safe to play the ♡K. If East then returns a club, East can give you a club ruff when in with the ♠A. That gives you +500 for a top board.

If West continues with a club at trick 2, dummy wins and South pitches the heart loser on dummy's top diamonds. You should then collect 200, which will still be a good score.

51. Dealer South : East-West vulnerable

```
                    ♠ ---
                    ♡ J 6 5 4
                    ◇ Q 9 6 3 2
                    ♣ J 7 5 4
W    N    E    S                      ♠ A Q 7 6
               1♣                     ♡ Q 8 7 2
1♠   Dble 4♠   5♡                     ◇ A 10 8
P    P    Dble End                    ♣ 9 6
```

West leads the ♠2, ruffed in dummy. Declarer plays the ♣J: nine – ace – three and the ♠10, nine, ruffed. After the ♣4 to the ten and queen, West plays the ♡K. South takes the ace and comes out with the ♣K. West discards and East ruffs. East switches to the ◇8. West takes the ◇K and returns the ◇J, which wins, followed by the ♠K: ♣7 - ♠Q - ♡3. South plays a club winner and ruffs with the ♡J. What should East do?   *Solution on page 86.*

52. Dealer North : East-West vulnerable

```
                    ♠ 4
                    ♡ 10 6
                    ◇ K Q 8 5 4 3 2
                    ♣ A 6 2
```

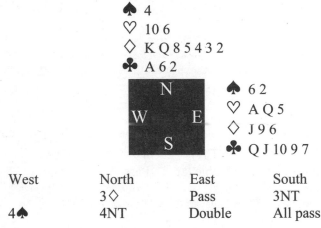

```
                                     ♠ 6 2
                                     ♡ A Q 5
                                     ◇ J 9 6
                                     ♣ Q J 10 9 7
```

West	North	East	South
	3◇	Pass	3NT
4♠	4NT	Double	All pass

West leads the ♡3. Plan East's defence.
          Solution on page 87.

53. Dealer North : East-West vulnerable

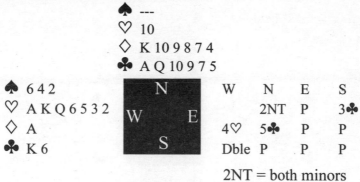

$\spadesuit$ ---
$\heartsuit$ 10
$\diamondsuit$ K 10 9 8 7 4
$\clubsuit$ A Q 10 9 7 5

$\spadesuit$ 6 4 2
$\heartsuit$ A K Q 6 5 3 2
$\diamondsuit$ A
$\clubsuit$ K 6

W	N	E	S
	2NT	P	3$\clubsuit$
4$\heartsuit$	5$\clubsuit$	P	P
Dble	P	P	P

2NT = both minors

West leads the $\heartsuit$A: ten – four – seven. What next?
Solution on page 88.

54. Dealer East : Nil vulnerable

$\spadesuit$ J 4
$\heartsuit$ ---
$\diamondsuit$ A K 7 6 5 3
$\clubsuit$ Q J 8 4 3

$\spadesuit$ A 8 5 3
$\heartsuit$ A J 9 8 6
$\diamondsuit$ ---
$\clubsuit$ A K 7 5

West	North	East	South
		1$\heartsuit$	Pass
2$\heartsuit$	2NT (1)	4$\heartsuit$	Pass
Pass	Double (2)	Pass	5$\diamondsuit$
Pass	Pass	Double	All pass

(1) Minors   (2) Asking partner to defend or to sacrifice

West leads the $\heartsuit$K, ruffed. South plays the $\diamondsuit$A: $\heartsuit$9 – $\diamondsuit$2 – $\diamondsuit$4, followed by the $\clubsuit$Q: king – six – nine. What next?

Solution on page 89.

51. Board 3, Round of 32, Rosenblum (World Open Teams), 2010

Contract: 5♡ doubled
Lead: ♠2

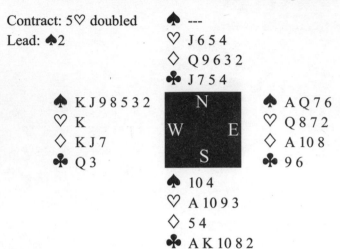

After the first nine tricks as described, these cards remain:

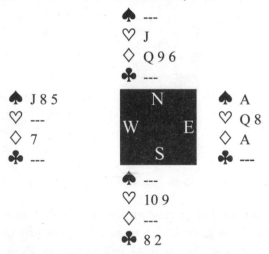

South played the ♣8 and ruffed with the ♡J. East over-ruffed and South had the rest for three down, −500 and +3 Imps. East should discard the ♠A instead of over-ruffing. Now East makes two more tricks for +800 and +5 Imps. Constant concentration is vital.

52. Board 83, quarter-finals, World Open Teams, 2012:

Contract: 4NT doubled
Lead: ♡3

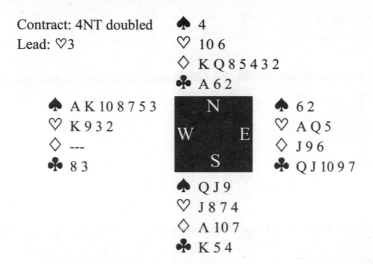

♠ 4
♡ 10 6
♢ K Q 8 5 4 3 2
♣ A 6 2

♠ A K 10 8 7 5 3
♡ K 9 3 2
♢ ---
♣ 8 3

♠ 6 2
♡ A Q 5
♢ J 9 6
♣ Q J 10 9 7

♠ Q J 9
♡ J 8 7 4
♢ Λ 10 7
♣ K 5 4

For North-South to sacrifice was a sound move, as 4♠ is unbeatable. Had they saved in 5♢, the cost would be 300 at most. Playing in 4NT doubled put the pressure on East-West to do the right thing. If West leads a low spade, South can quickly claim ten tricks.

West's lead of a low heart was a good start. East could play ♡A, ♡Q and a third heart to give East-West six tricks and +500. In practice East won with the ♡A, South playing ♡4, and switched to the ♠6: queen, king. West cashed the ♡K and then paused for a long time. Finally West played a third heart to East's queen and East returned the ♠2. The defence thus took ten tricks, +1700.

East should be aware that to stay in 4NT doubled, South would have a sound spade stopper, Q-J-x or K-10-x , not just Q-x-x or K-x-x. In that case East would need two entries to push spades through declarer and the only quick entries would be in hearts. East should play the ♡Q at trick 1 and switch to the ♠6. Now the defence is easy for partner. West did well to find the right sequence of plays, but East could have saved West a lot of anxiety.

53. Board 2, semi-finals, Baze Seniors Teams (USA), 2013

Contract: 5♣ doubled
Lead: ♡A

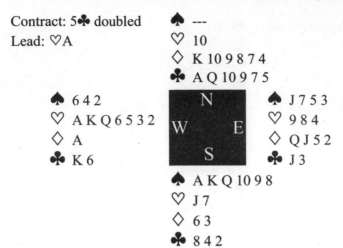

♠ ---
♡ 10
◇ K 10 9 8 7 4
♣ A Q 10 9 7 5

♠ 6 4 2
♡ A K Q 6 5 3 2
◇ A
♣ K 6

♠ J 7 5 3
♡ 9 8 4
◇ Q J 5 2
♣ J 3

♠ A K Q 10 9 8
♡ J 7
◇ 6 3
♣ 8 4 2

From West's point of view, the bidding sounded like North was taking a sacrifice. It is always a pleasure when the opponents misread a bid as a sacrifice when you were planning to bid it anyway, with the hope and expectation of making.

Incredibly, declarer finished with – would you believe? – twelve tricks, +650. How could that happen? At trick 2 West erred seriously by switching to the ♣6. Declarer finessed the ♣Q, followed by the ♣A. Declarer can now succeed by playing a low diamond, but that is double dummy. Hoping for the ♠J to drop in three rounds, South played the ♣5 to the ♣8. On this trick East became an accessory after the crime by discarding the ♠3. Could it hurt to discard a heart? Declarer now played six rounds of spades, discarding all of dummy's diamonds.

West should never have given East the chance to make a mistake. At trick 2 West should play the ◇A, then the ♡K or ♡Q. When declarer ruffs this, he is locked in dummy. West must now score the ♣K. This defence fails only if South began with one heart.

54. Round 2, Board 17, European Champions' Cup, 2014

Contract: 5♢ doubled
Lead: ♡K

♠ J 4
♡ ---
♢ A K 7 6 5 3
♣ Q J 8 4 3

♠ Q 7 6 2
♡ K Q 5 2
♢ Q 9 4
♣ 9 2

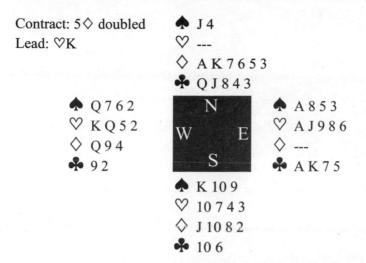

♠ A 8 5 3
♡ A J 9 8 6
♢ ---
♣ A K 7 5

♠ K 10 9
♡ 10 7 4 3
♢ J 10 8 2
♣ 10 6

East-West would have no trouble making 4♡ and so you need to score as much as possible in penalties. After the ♡K lead, ruffed, the ♢A from dummy and the ♣Q: king – six - nine, East knows from West's ♣9 that declarer still has the ♣10. Declarer's failure to continue trumps is telling. It strongly suggests West has a trump holding that cannot be readily eliminated.

East could play a heart, forcing dummy to ruff. There can be little harm in that, but also probably not much good. A low spade is not a good idea. It will not hurt if West has the king, but if South has the king, South will hardly misguess. After all, West raised only to 2♡ and has led the ♡K. The ♠A is sensible. If West has the king, fine. If not, no real harm has been done. When West discourages a spade continuation, East can cash the ♣K and play another club. This will create a trump trick for West and give East-West 300.

At the table East played a low spade at trick 4. South rose with the ♠K and led the ♢J, queen, king. A diamond to the ten drew West's trump and declarer had ten tricks for –100. In two other matches, the defence also took only three tricks against 5♢ doubled.

55. Dealer East : East-West vulnerable

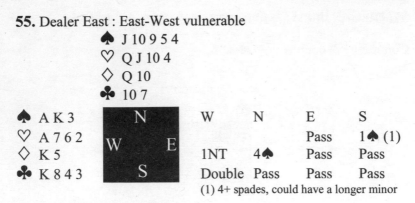

♠ J 10 9 5 4
♥ Q J 10 4
♦ Q 10
♣ 10 7

♠ A K 3
♥ A 7 6 2
♦ K 5
♣ K 8 4 3

W	N	E	S
		Pass	1♠ (1)
1NT	4♠	Pass	Pass
Double	Pass	Pass	Pass

(1) 4+ spades, could have a longer minor

West leads ♠A, ♠K and ♠3. East follows once and then discards two clubs. Declarer wins the third spade in dummy and plays the ♦Q: four – seven – king. What next?   *Solution on page 92.*

56. Dealer East : East-West vulnerable

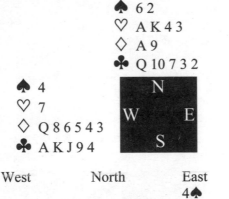

♠ 6 2
♥ A K 4 3
♦ A 9
♣ Q 10 7 3 2

♠ 4
♥ 7
♦ Q 8 6 5 4 3
♣ A K J 9 4

West	North	East	South
		4♠	Pass
Pass	Double (1)	Pass	5♥
Double	Pass	Pass	Pass

(1) Primarily for takeout

West leads the ♣K: two – eight – five. Unsure of the location of the missing club, West shifts to the ♠4: two – queen – ten. East continues with the ♠K, ♠J from South. What should West play?

Solution on page 93.

57. Dealer North : Nil vulnerable

♠ Q 8 6 5
♡ 2
♢ 6 5 2
♣ K 10 7 6 4

♠ K J 7 3
♡ A 9
♢ K J 4
♣ A Q 8 5

West	North	East	South
	Pass	1♣	4♡
Double (1)	Pass	Pass	Pass

(1) Primarily for takeout

West leads the ♣9: four – queen – jack. East plays the ♣A: two – three – six. How would you continue as East?

Solution on page 94.

58. Dealer North : Both vulnerable

♠ 4
♡ K J 9 8 6 2
♢ 4 3
♣ J 10 8 2

♠ J 10 9 2
♡ ---
♢ 10 8 7 6
♣ K 6 5 4 3

West	North	East	South
	2♡	Pass	6♢
Pass	Pass	Double	Redouble
Pass	Pass	Pass	

Lead: ♡4 – two – ♢6 – ♡Q. What should East play next?

Solution on page 95.

55. Board 85, final of the World Seniors' Teams, 2008

Contract: 4♠ doubled
Lead: ♠A

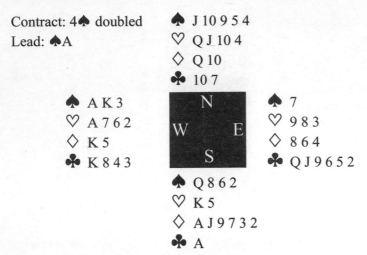

♠ J 10 9 5 4
♥ Q J 10 4
♦ Q 10
♣ 10 7

♠ A K 3
♥ A 7 6 2
♦ K 5
♣ K 8 4 3

♠ 7
♥ 9 8 3
♦ 8 6 4
♣ Q J 9 6 5 2

♠ Q 8 6 2
♥ K 5
♦ A J 9 7 3 2
♣ A

West began with three rounds of spades against 4♠ doubled. South won the third round in dummy and ran the ♦Q to West's king. West switched to a low club. That was fatal. South won and played off the diamonds, discarding all of dummy's hearts. He could then ruff two hearts in dummy and a club in hand for +590.

At the other table East-West bid to 5♣ undoubled. The result was one off, USA –100, but +10 Imps on the board. Japan won the final by 202-200, but had they lost, Japan's West would have regretted the club switch at trick 5 against 4♠ doubled.

West should not need any help from partner. After winning with the ♦K, West should play the ♥A. On the actual layout that takes the contract one down. If East happened to have the ♥K, it would be two down. What is the worst scenario for the ♥A switch? If South is void in hearts and ruffs the ♥A, it would be with South's last trump. You would not be exposing East's ♥K to a ruffing finesse. If there is even the slightest risk that the opponents' contract might make, your first priority is to make sure you defeat it. You can worry about two down after you have it one down.

56. Board 1, Rosenblum (World Open Teams) semi-finals 2014

Contract: 5♡ doubled
Lead: ♣K

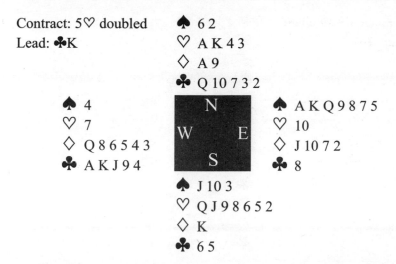

♠ 6 2
♡ A K 4 3
♢ A 9
♣ Q 10 7 3 2

♠ 4
♡ 7
♢ Q 8 6 5 4 3
♣ A K J 9 4

♠ A K Q 9 8 7 5
♡ 10
♢ J 10 7 2
♣ 8

♠ J 10 3
♡ Q J 9 8 6 5 2
♢ K
♣ 6 5

After ♣K and the ♠4 to the queen, East played the ♠K and West discarded the ♢6. East switched to the ♢J. Declarer won with the ♢K and drew trumps. He then discarded his club loser on dummy's ♢A. The result was one down, –100. That was a superb outcome for North-South since 4♠ could not be defeated.

The contract should go two down. West should ruff the second spade and play the ♣A. What hope did the defence have for a diamond trick? Would East open 4♠ in first seat with seven or eight spades to the A-K-Q and the ♢K, too? There was further evidence. How did East play the spades? Queen first, then the king. With the ♢K, East could play the ♠A first and the ♠K next as suit-preference for diamonds. The clues were all there for West.

At the other table South was in 6♡ doubled, saving against 5♠, which can be defeated. The defence went the same way against 6♡. Again West failed to ruff the second spade and took declarer two down instead of three down. In the MConnell (Women's) and the Rand (Seniors), two tables were in 5♡ doubled. Both Wests began with the ♣K, but again the result was also only one down.

57. Board 45, Rosenblum (World Open Teams) final, 2014

Contract: 4♡ doubled   ♠ Q 8 6 5
Lead: ♣9   ♡ 2
                           ◇ 6 5 2
                           ♣ K 10 7 6 4

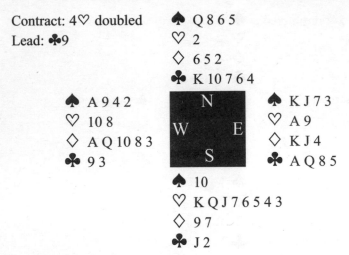

♠ A 9 4 2   ♠ K J 7 3
♡ 10 8   ♡ A 9
◇ A Q 10 8 3   ◇ K J 4
♣ 9 3   ♣ A Q 8 5

                           ♠ 10
                           ♡ K Q J 7 6 5 4 3
                           ◇ 9 7
                           ♣ J 2

After East takes the ♣Q and ♣A, there is a temptation to play a
third club, but if you do South will simply discard a loser. East has
18 HCP, dummy has 5 HCP and South will have good hearts.
Given West's takeout double, possibly committing East-West to
4♠ or the five-level, can West have less than the ♠A and ◇A?

East should switch to the ◇4. West can win, cash the ♠A and
return a low diamond to East's ◇K (indicated by the ◇4 switch).
Now a club will create a fourth defensive trick. The order was not
the same, but the result was, when Claudio Nunes, West, and
Fulvio Fantoni were defending: East won the first club and
already switched to the ◇4. West won and cashed the ♠A. East
played the ♠3, reverse count to show an even number. West
cashed the ◇A and played his second club. East won and returned
a club. South ruffed with ♡J and continued with the ♡Q to East's
ace. The next club promoted West's ♡10 for four down.

At the other table 5♡ doubled was four down after a heart lead. In
the McConnell Women's World Teams, 4♡ doubled was three
down, −500 once after a trump lead and once after the ♣9 lead.

58. Board 27, Rosenblum (World Open Teams) Round of 16, 2014

Contract: 6◇ redoubled
Lead: ♡4

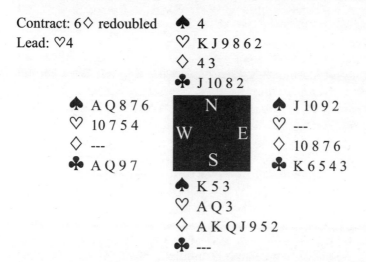

```
              ♠ 4
              ♡ K J 9 8 6 2
              ◇ 4 3
              ♣ J 10 8 2
♠ A Q 8 7 6           ♠ J 10 9 2
♡ 10 7 5 4            ♡ ---
◇ ---                 ◇ 10 8 7 6
♣ A Q 9 7            ♣ K 6 5 4 3
              ♠ K 5 3
              ♡ A Q 3
              ◇ A K Q J 9 5 2
              ♣ ---
```

This was an exciting board in almost every match. At one table it went 2♡ : 6 ◇, all pass. West led the ♠A on which East played the ten, suit-preference for hearts. West switched to a heart. East ruffed, one down. At the other table North opened a multi 2◇. After a 2NT inquiry, South ended in 6♡. Played by South, 6♡ is unbeatable, North-South +1430 and +17 Imps.

In another match, North-South also had the 2♡ : 6◇, all pass auction. West led the ♣A, N-S +1390. At the other table North began with a multi 2◇ and South ended in 6♡, +1430, +1 Imp.

In a third match, North passed, South opened 1◇, East-West found their spade fit and South later bid 6◇. This could be beaten, but West saved in 6♠ doubled, played by East. He ruffed the ◇A lead in dummy, ruffed a heart and played a club. If South ruffed, the slam could make and so South pitched the ♡A. After ♣Q, declarer ruffed a heart and led another club. South discarded and the ♣A won. When East ruffed the third heart, South over-ruffed and played a trump. East had two more losers, two off, N-S +500.

At the other table West also saved in 6♠ doubled, but he was declarer. A misdefence allowed West to escape for one down −200 and +7 imps.

In another match, both sides were in 6◇ doubled. With South declarer, West led the ♠A. East played the ♠9, but West shifted to the ♣A, North-South +1540. At the other table, with North declarer, East led the ♠10, king, ace. West won and continued with the ♠Q, North-South 1540, no swing.

The biggest swing occurred when West led the ♠A against South's 6◇ and switched to a heart for +100. At the other table North was in 7♡ doubled. When East led the ♣3, declarer made all the tricks, +2470 and +21 Imps.

Now to Problem 58: When East made a Lightner double of 6◇ to ask for a heart lead and South redoubled, West led the ♡4. East ruffed, South played the ♡Q and East needed to play a spade at trick 2. In practice East switched to the ◇7, aiming to cut down ruffs in dummy, North-South +1830.

There are sufficient clues for East to find the spade switch. South's ♡Q will not be from A-Q doubleton. With that, South would play the ♡A in order to reach dummy. (Indeed, South should have played the ♡A, not the ♡Q.)

With three or four hearts, South has no need to ruff any losers in dummy. South will have five heart tricks, plus the presumably long and solid diamonds. With first-round control in spades and clubs, South will not be defeated. If South lacks a black ace, West might have tried to cash that before giving East the heart ruff. If West has both black aces, then South must have a void. Where will that void be? It will almost certainly be in clubs, not spades.

When the world's top players fail to find the best defence, there is hope for us all.